THE LAST GODFATHER

THE LAST GODFATHER

THE RISE AND FALL OF JOEY MASSINO

SIMON CRITTLE

BERKLEY BOOKS, NEW YORK

THE BERKLEY PUBLISHING GROUP
Published by the Penguin Group
Penguin Group (USA) Inc.
375 Hudson Street, New York, New York 10014, USA
Penguin Group (Canada), 90 Eglinton Avenue East, Suite 700, Toronto, Ontario M4P 2Y3, Canada
(a division of Pearson Penguin Canada Inc.)
Penguin Books Ltd., 80 Strand, London WC2R 0RL, England
Penguin Group Ireland, 25 St. Stephen's Green, Dublin 2, Ireland (a division of Penguin Books Ltd.)
Penguin Group (Australia), 250 Camberwell Road, Camberwell, Victoria 3124, Australia
(a division of Pearson Australia Group Pty. Ltd.)
Penguin Books India Pvt. Ltd., 11 Community Centre, Panchsheel Park, New Delhi—110 017, India
Penguin Group (NZ), Cnr. Airborne and Rosedale Roads, Albany, Auckland 1310, New Zealand
(a division of Pearson New Zealand Ltd.)
Penguin Books (South Africa) (Pty.) Ltd., 24 Sturdee Avenue, Rosebank, Johannesburg 2196, South
Africa

Penguin Books Ltd., Registered Offices: 80 Strand, London WC2R 0RL, England

THE LAST GODFATHER

A Berkley Book / published by arrangement with the author

PRINTING HISTORY
Berkley mass-market edition / March 2006

ISBN: 0-425-20939-3

BERKLEY®
Berkley Books are published by The Berkley Publishing Group,
a division of Penguin Group (USA) Inc.,
375 Hudson Street, New York, New York 10014.
BERKLEY is a registered trademark of Penguin Group (USA) Inc.
The "B" design is a trademark belonging to Penguin Group (USA) Inc.

PRINTED IN THE UNITED STATES OF AMERICA

10 9 8 7 6 5

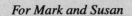

For Mark and Susan

For all their assistance, I would like to acknowledge James Elder, Jami Schievelbein, Kati Cornell Smith, David Smith and Samantha Ward.

Foreword

by Joe Pistone

I heard the mob had a $500,000 price on my head, so I don't use my real name much anymore. To keep one step ahead, I use several aliases, which are printed on everything from my driver's license to my checkbook. Living in hiding is a legacy from my days as an undercover agent working for the FBI. I had a false name then, too. You might have heard of it: Donnie Brasco. They used it for the title of a movie. Before, it was what the wiseguys called me.

I know a thing or two about wiseguys. For five years, I pretended to be one of them. I breathed their air, ate dinner in their homes, and was privy to their crimes. Having grown up as a street guy in Paterson, New Jersey, I was, as they say, "street smart." I knew wiseguys in my old neighborhood, knew how they talked and walked. So I was comfortable in the role of Brasco. Life in the mob was about eating well, dressing sharp and planning scores. I got respect from people who thought I was a gangster. But I spent most of my time gathering evidence and trying not to get killed. If they'd ever suspected me, or worse, mistaken me for a rat, I wouldn't be writing this now.

People say I had a lot to do with killing off the mob. That's only half right. Yeah, I put a lot of bad guys behind bars, but the mob isn't dead yet. As long as there is crime in New York, bad guys will try to organize it. That said, the mob isn't what it used to be. Wiseguys today don't take pride in their tradition. They are four and five generations removed from the old ways. *Omertà* (Italian for "conspiracy of silence") used to mean something. These guys today, they get caught and right away they start singing. In the old days, if you caught them, you caught them. End of story, say no more.

There was only one big-name wiseguy who held on to the old traditions. His name was Joey Massino. I knew him in the old days—he was the last of the old-time gangsters. Joey wasn't out prancing around like John Gotti. He was never around, hitting the nightspots. He flew low under the radar. But make no mistake: Joey was a stone-cold killer. He was a greatly feared figure even in my day. His reputation on the street was as big as he was, and Joey was a big guy.

But he also had a sense of humor. After I surfaced from undercover assignment in the mob, I testified against Joey in court. One day at the trial, he said to me, "Hey, Donnie, who's gonna play me in the movie?" I said, "Joey, we're having a problem. We can't find an actor fat enough." But Joey had the last laugh. He was acquitted and went on to become boss of the Bonanno Crime Family.

The Bonanno Family was the family I infiltrated. I hooked up with a crew run by a guy named Dominick "Sonny Black" Napolitano out of Brooklyn. Sonny and Joey were closely aligned, and both made their names as truck hijackers. At the time, the Family was gripped by an internal power struggle, and in 1981 three captains from one of the warring factions got whacked. We now know Joey ordered the hits with Sonny by his side.

With bullets flying in all directions, my supervisors decided to yank me off the street, and we quietly informed the Bonannos they'd been compromised. For my protection, it was better to let them know I was an agent and not a rat. Not long after, Sonny disappeared. His body turned up in a shallow grave on Staten Island a few years later. The word on the street was that he'd been killed for allowing me to worm my way into his crew and humiliate the Family.

Being partly responsible for Sonny's death has always been a sore point for me. I went undercover to put wiseguys in prison, not to get them killed. I always hoped Sonny's killers would be brought to justice. I had to wait more than twenty years for that. It was Joey who ordered the hit. In

2004, he was convicted of the murder—along with six others—and sentenced to life in prison. Good riddance, I say. Not only are New York's streets that much safer, but for me personally, his conviction closes the book on one of my false names, Donnie Brasco.

PROLOGUE

After the guilty verdicts were read, Joseph Massino turned, looked at his wife, Josephine, and shrugged. Everything was lost. The boss of one of New York's five Mafia Families, the Bonannos, had been convicted of seven murders and hit with a forfeiture demand of roughly $10 million. He also faced the death penalty in an upcoming trial and, given what had just happened, conviction looked certain.

As Massino was led out the side door of the Brooklyn federal courtroom, Josephine sat frozen with disbelief, her tight-fitting dark pantsuit, tinted glasses and perfectly stiff brown bob belying her complete horror. Positioned directly behind her was the leather-faced *New*

York Post reporter Steve Dunleavy. He'd been courting the gangster's wife for weeks with a string of sympathetic columns. Now the Australian moved in for the kill, so close she could smell his breath. "Josephine," he said, "wanna make a comment?" When she said nothing, her portly minder glanced at Dunleavy and shook his head. By then, the courtroom had emptied. Josephine slowly rose and turned for the door. When she reached the hallway, the media pack pounced, following her to the elevator bank. As is the custom, the prosecution team, standing nearby, was waiting for the defendant's family to board the elevator before taking the next one. The press wasn't so kind—half a dozen reporters, including myself, crowded in behind her. Before the doors closed, Josephine's minder reached in, took her by the arm and pulled her back into the hallway, leaving us to descend empty-handed.

Outside the courthouse, the government was preparing to give a press conference. We assembled beneath the microphone with TV cameras at our backs. At the same time, Josephine and her entourage exited the building and strode past us, staring straight ahead. Dunleavy followed her across Brooklyn's Cadman Plaza at a safe twenty paces behind. We lost sight of them as the conference began. "Joseph Massino reigned over the Bonanno Crime Family's bloody history for more than two decades," U.S. Attorney Roslynn Mauskopf boomed into the microphone. "He was the last boss walking the streets of New York. This conviction marks an important step in our fight against organized crime."

The big news, however, was unfolding back upstairs. What nobody noticed as they were leaving the courtroom was Massino, sixty-one, whispering in the ear of a court officer. "I need to talk to the judge," he said. Under the circumstances, it was an extraordinary request. Nevertheless, the officer obliged, and instead of being handed back to the Marshall Service, the obese mobster was whisked into the chambers of Judge Nicholas Garaufis. For the past ten weeks of the trial, Massino's attorney had vehemently denied that his client was guilty. Now, in the judge's corner office, with sweeping views of the Manhattan Bridge and the Empire State Building before him, Massino made an incredible admission. "I'm ready to talk."

Not even Judge Garaufis could fathom the magnitude of what Joe Massino would eventually reveal. The Bonanno boss would lead authorities to hidden graves of two of his victims and reveal an alleged plot to kill a federal prosecutor—the one slated to go up against Massino in his next trial. But there in the chambers, the judge did realize something monumental was happening. It wasn't just that a Mafia boss was actually volunteering to talk—though that in itself was a first in New York. This was Joseph Massino, the last Five Family boss walking the streets, and arguably the most powerful criminal in America. The man who ruthlessly brought the Bonanno Crime Family back from the brink of extinction. The man who taught his organization to value loyalty, honor and secrecy above all else.

It would be another six months until the news of Massino's deal—confession, in exchange for escaping the death penalty on the outstanding murder charge— would make headlines. But on June 30, 2004, in Judge Garaufis's chambers, history was made. The Last Godfather broke his sacred vow of silence.

This book is the first inside account of the chilling events and breathtaking betrayal that led up to that moment.

ONE

DEATH ELIGIBLE

On the last day of his life, Gerlando Sciascia combed his wiry crop of gray hair into his signature pompadour style. Two silver stripes extended from his temples to the back of his ears, where they blended into the salt-and-pepper mass on the top and rear of his head. Saving the best for last, he stroked his thick, black sideburns into place so that they formed sharp points, contoured to the line of his jaw. Sciascia then donned a red Argyle sweater, gray slacks and a leather jacket. As usual, he looked immaculate.

The hair was the most striking feature of an otherwise ordinary-looking man. Sciascia, sixty-six, was of medium height and build, with a long, thin nose and little dark eyes. He lived in an elegant home in the Bronx with his wife and adoring daughter. He seemed ordinary enough too—when people asked him what he did for a living, he told them he was in construction. But in reality, he conducted most of his wheeling and dealing out of a jewelry store on East Tremont Avenue. As his hairstyle suggested, Gerlando Sciascia was anything but ordinary.

When Sciascia arrived at his store on March 18, 1999, he found a message waiting for him. He made a note of it on a scrap of paper: "Pat D 79." Sciascia had been summoned to a meeting on the Upper East Side (the "79" stood for Seventy-ninth Street in Manhattan). He took the Cross Bronx Expressway, drove across the East River and headed south on the Harlem River Drive. He parked his car and walked one block to Café 79, a grimy diner at the corner of First Avenue and Seventy-ninth Street. He entered alone, and took a seat in one of the gray vinyl booths.

Sciascia thought he was there for a greasy meal and conversation with a business colleague. What he didn't know was that his bullet-ridden corpse would eventually bring about the downfall of one of the most feared and elusive figures in the New York City Mafia—an organization many (incorrectly) believed was dead.

With bleary eyes, they filed into Brooklyn's six-story federal courthouse in April 2004. They were ordinary, hardworking people: cabdrivers, nurses, clerical workers, teachers. They had kids in school, bills to pay and headaches to treat when they got home. None of the 422 people knew any of the others, but they all shared a common condition: they were the members of the jury pool.

The first batch of jurors was ushered into the building's enormous Ceremonial Courtroom at 11 a.m. Some exchanged curious whispers; others wore puzzled expressions. Most just stared blankly at the sixties' décor as if resigned to their fate. The side door banged and a command to "All rise!" rang out as Judge Nicholas Garaufis swept into the room, his black robes flapping behind him. A mid-sized, pale man with neatly parted gray hair and a warm, pudgy face, Judge Garaufis took his seat at the top level of the bench. He peered through his metal-rimmed spectacles at a short pile of documents before looking up at his jury pool with a broad smile and bidding them good morning. He politely began explaining that they'd been called to perform the last great duty of a democratic society. Then, without pause or theatrics, he dropped the first bombshell.

"You are here as potential jurors in the case of the *United States v. Joseph Massino,* the alleged boss of the Bonanno Crime Family." The jury pool fell silent—as New Yorkers, they needed no explanation. They shifted uncomfortably on their benches as the judge read off the charges, including extortion, narcotics distribution and seven murders (Massino was charged with the murder of Gerlando Sciascia in a separate indictment). "The trial," he said, "is expected to take up to six weeks." Moving quickly along, the judge directed the potential jurors' attention to a heavyset man sitting quietly at the front of the room. Until then, the jury pool had barely noticed him among the handful of lawyers seated nearby. But there he was, in the flesh: Joseph Massino.

Judge Garaufis asked the defendant to stand so that he could be introduced to the crowd. Wearing a steel-gray suit and a white open-necked shirt, Massino rose, turned to the pool and waved an awkward hello. At that moment, he looked oddly normal—just like a regular guy. But the government knew better. In a previous court session, the judge had granted the prosecution a motion to keep the jury anonymous. "The identity of potential and seated jurors will be kept confidential," Judge Garaufis told the pool. "The final jury will be escorted to and from the courthouse each day." The FBI knew Joe Massino was no regular guy.

Over the next few weeks, the pool was narrowed down by the prosecuting and defense attorneys. The potential jurors filled out a thirty-eight-page questionnaire, which asked questions like "Do you believe there is an actual entity called the Mafia? Have you heard of *The Sopranos*?" More often than not, the answer was yes. A mother of two who worked in customer service and was called back for questioning broke down in tears saying she feared for her safety. "I've seen the movies," she sobbed, "the Mafia can make evidence disappear." Another woman said her father was actually gunned down by the mob. Prosecutors looked into her story, and it turned out her father was in fact Bartholomew "Bobby" Borriello, once a trusted aide to John Gotti, who was shot dead in his Brooklyn driveway in 1991. (The woman was excused.) And so it continued. After two mind-numbing weeks, Massino's jury pool had been whittled down to four men and eight women.

Joseph C. Massino was born on January 10, 1943. A Queens native, he first made his name in the Mafia as a truck hijacker, and quickly rose through the ranks of the Bonanno Crime Family. Massino became the driving force behind the resurgence of the Family, after long periods of turbulence in the 1960s, '70s and '80s. He would eventually become the kingpin of an organized crime operation that spanned international borders.

In the early years of his career, Joey Massino spent as much time working in commercial kitchens as behind the wheel of a stolen truck. An accomplished cook, he prepared food in delicatessens, industrial kitchens, catering halls and restaurants. With a stick of gum in his mouth and grease up to his elbows, he'd slice, knead and fry, happy to take the time alone to think—he made his best decisions standing over a bubbling stove. One of his favorite pastimes was dreaming up new recipes and testing them out. The proof was in the pudding of his enormous round belly. Massino was so wide around the middle—at one point, he weighed close to four hundred pounds—that he waddled instead of walked. However, a man of his stature could waddle free from ridicule. His enormous shoulders and tree-trunk neck were actually in proportion to his midsection, so the overall effect of his appearance was that of a fearsome bull. He slicked his dark hair up and back, exposing his large forehead and fleshy cheeks. The deep furrows of his brow and his finger-thick eyebrows gave him a permanently dark expression.

Massino got his start in the catering business working for a spry man he called "Unc." Of course, the man wasn't really his uncle, but you could say both men were apples from the same tree. "Unc" was in fact the notorious Bonanno Family gangster Philip "Rusty" Rastelli. Massino went to work for his catering business after dropping out of Grover Cleveland High School in nearby Ridgewood. Standing at only 5'8", Rastelli was a reputed narcotics trafficker, loan shark, labor racketeer and murderer who, among other crimes, was suspected of killing his wife. He also ran a lucrative gambling business out of a fleet of silver catering trucks (lunch wagons or "roach coaches," as the drivers called them). As soon as he was able, Massino followed in his mentor's footsteps, buying his own catering truck and route. The sight of Joe Massino, by then a true mountain of a man, hunched over the wheel of his little silver truck, speeding between truck stops and factories in Queens, became a familiar sight to the FBI agents assigned to keep tabs on him. "One for you, and one for me," they would joke about the cakes he sold.

While Massino was making a name for himself driving his lunch wagon and stealing trucks, the Family was being led by its namesake, Joseph "Joe Bananas" Bonanno. The stocky Sicilian was appointed boss at the tender age of twenty-six when Lucky Luciano incorporated New York's Five Families in 1931, at the end of the great mob wars over bootleg alcohol rackets during Prohibition. Bonanno ruled the Family for almost forty years, was said to have been courted by the Kennedys, and had extensive casino holdings in the city's garment district. As a founding member of the Mafia Commission, a group representing all five Families, he believed in the old-world Sicilian code of honor and despised his fast-living American-born counterparts. "He came from a culture and tradition that taught people what was right from wrong," Bonanno's son Bill said in an interview. "When they tried to transfer it to this country, that tradition got diluted by the marketplace mentality of American society. The family ties and connections, the trust, the loyalty and obedience—the glue that held us together—that's not there anymore."

By the early sixties, Bonanno's stock of trust and loyalty was running out. He had powerful enemies, ranging from Attorney General Robert Kennedy to mob rival Carlo Gambino. To buy time, Bonanno faked his own kidnapping in 1964. He resurfaced in 1966, but was never able to regain control of the Family. He eventually retired to Tucson, Arizona, where he penned an autobiography in 1983, parting with his precious code of honor. (In a strangely poetic twist, then–Manhattan U.S. Attorney Rudy Giuliani would later use the book as evidence the Commission actually did exist, and jail four of the five Family bosses, as well as Bonanno, in a landmark trial in the 1980s.) Bonanno died in 2002 at age ninety-seven. His son promptly posted his Tucson home on eBay.

After the so-called "Banana War," when Family factions battled for control after Bonanno's retirement, Rastelli emerged as the new boss. His reign was anything but easy. In 1975, he was busted for extortion and sentenced to ten years in prison. Around the same time, Joseph Bonanno's underboss, Carmine Galante, one of the most ruthless and bloodthirsty gangsters of the era, was released from prison after a twelve-year stint for heroin trafficking. He snatched control of the Family in spite of Rastelli's standing. Galante's murderous influence over the Bonanno organization came to a spectacular end when he was rubbed out in 1979, as he ate lunch on the patio of Joe and Mary's Restaurant in Bushwick, Brooklyn. The photo of Galante lying dead, a burning cigar still pressed between his lips, is one of the most famous images of New York City's Mafia in action.

Rastelli remained official boss of the Family until his death in 1991, but it was Joe Massino—Rastelli's most powerful captain—who'd been running the Family since the early eighties. Massino had quietly emerged as one of the most feared figures in New York's criminal underworld. (So great was his power that he was actually named boss of the Family while he was serving a short prison sentence in the early nineties for a labor racketeering scheme involving the Teamsters Local 814.)

At the height of his power, Massino had more than 100 made men under his command. His organization's tentacles stretched from New York to Canada and all the way back to the Sicilian motherland, and extended deep into truck hijacking, extortion, illegal sports betting operations, stock market schemes and loan-sharking. It was Massino who quietly resurrected the Family after the shock of the Donnie Brasco episode (in which undercover FBI agent Joseph Pistone spent five years posing as a jewel thief named Donnie Brasco within the Bonanno family. Pistone's testimony later sent two hundred gangsters to prison.) Afterward, the humiliated Bonannos were booted from the Five Families national crime syndicate and left for dead. But with brains and brute force, Joey Massino brought them back to life.

Lawmen often compared Massino to late Gambino Family boss John Gotti, describing them as self-made "blue-collar" gangsters who were schooled on the street. True, they both began as truck hijackers and operated in the same part of New York. They were business associates, close friends and neighbors: they lived two blocks from each other in Howard Beach, Queens. But their most striking similarity was their use of fear as a weapon, deftly wielding it to control their lieutenants and terrify their rivals. Like Gotti, Massino was a stone-cold killer, a treacherous and calculating boss who thought nothing of whacking an associate who no longer served a purpose. According to testimony, he once lured a man who was a partner in a cigarette smuggling ring to a second-story apartment in Queens on the pretense of settling a debt. When the man reached the top of the stairs, Massino and an accomplice knocked him down with a sharp blow to the head. An autopsy later revealed the victim had been shot six times: in the right eye, chin, left side of his jaw, chest, neck and right thumb. The wound to the thumb was most likely a defensive injury sustained when the man tried to block the fire to his face.

Massino and Gotti might both have been feared, but that's where their similarities ended. Gotti's ego was as big as his reputation—he wore expensive suits, courted celebrities, and bantered with TV reporters. Eventually, he became a victim of the sound of his own voice, after he was caught on a wiretap and jailed. He died in prison of throat cancer, unable to say a word. By contrast, Massino shunned the limelight, particularly after he was released from prison in 1993. After that point, he was rarely seen in public: he stopped going to weddings and wakes, and moved only between his home, his businesses and CasaBlanca, the restaurant he owned in Queens. He went so far as to order his men never to utter his name in conversation, and instead tug one of their ears to indicate they were talking about him. It was a touch of theater he borrowed from Genovese Family boss Vincent "The Chin" Gigante, whose henchmen used to tap their chins to signal their boss.

The source of Massino's power was the fact that you didn't know him. In under a decade, he turned the Bonanno Family into the most powerful criminal organization in America, quietly outpacing the earning ability of the better-known Gambino and Genovese Families. (One Bonanno turncoat put the Family holdings at roughly $100 million when he was arrested in 2002.) One by one, Massino's counterparts fell, sentenced to lifelong prison terms or reduced to tabloid fodder: Carmine "Junior" Perisco, the Colombo boss, got one hundred years, and Gigante ended up wandering the streets of Greenwich Village in a bathrobe and slippers. But Massino understood something they didn't. He was from a bygone era—the last of the old-world gangsters. He knew that the values of the Mafia—honor, respect and secrecy—were as much about self-preservation as tradition. Massino never wrote a book or did an interview. (When I asked him to give me one before his trial, he laughed and told me to "have a nice day.") At the time of his arrest in 2003, he was the only New York City boss not doing hard time or waiting to go on trial.

That made him the Last Godfather.

At 11 p.m. on the day he got the message in March 1999, Gerlando Sciascia (pronounced shaa-shaa) was found murdered in a dead-end street in the Bronx, across from a Baptist church. A witness described seeing a vehicle speed away and then noticing a body on its back. Sciascia's legs were splayed apart, and his head drooped to his right side. "He looked like someone's grandpa lying there," a bystander told the *New York Post*.

Sciascia had been shot five times at close range: two bullets to the head, one to the neck and two more to the left side of his torso. Upon closer examination, the detectives noticed dried blood on the side of his head, which was facing up, while the ground beneath the body was drip-free. They concluded that Sciascia had slumped facedown after being shot at an unknown location, and then been dumped in the street shortly afterward. His body was scooped up and taken to the Medical Examiner's Office. When the police plugged Sciascia's name into the computer, they were confronted with a file stretching back for decades. The bullet-ridden body in the morgue wasn't the average scum the cops scraped off the sidewalk: Sciascia was Mafiosi.

Gerlando Sciascia immigrated to the United States from Sicily in 1955, when he was nineteen. By the mid-1970s, he had been identified as a member of the Bonanno Family—one of the family "Zips," or Sicilian operatives. At the time of his death, Sciascia was the captain in charge of the Bonanno's plum northern outpost in Montreal, Family territory since the 1930s. Sciascia was known on the street as "George from Canada" and was considered a powerful figure on both sides of the border. He had more than a dozen Mafia soldiers under his command and was believed to have been an accomplice in at least four gangland murders.

Like many of the Sicilian Bonannos, most of whom were based in Brooklyn and Montreal, Sciascia had made a fortune trafficking heroin, which the Family had been smuggling into New York from Canada since the 1960s. His record was far from clean: in 1983, Sciascia was one of thirteen men—along with John Gotti's brother, Gene—named in a federal indictment as part of a smuggling ring alleged to have moved forty-six kilograms of heroin across the border. Sciascia ducked the subpoena and fled to Montreal, but he was arrested by the Royal Canadian Mounted Police in 1988 and extradited back to the States. Two years later, he won a miraculous acquittal. (It was later alleged that the trial was fixed. According to the infamous mob turncoat Sammy "The Bull" Gravano, Sciascia and his two codefendants got off because a juror was paid $10,000 to sway the panel.)

When word of Sciascia's murder reached the FBI, they didn't know what to make of it. The circumstances surrounding his death just didn't add up. For one thing, Mafia hit men usually disposed of dead bodies. Occasionally they'd turn up, but they'd be in such a state of decomposition, they'd be virtually unrecognizable. Not so with Sciascia—his killers just dumped him in the street. Secondly, investigators noted that after the murder, the Bonanno underboss, the acting consigliere and seven captains accompanied Sciascia's family to the wake, which indicated the hit had not been officially sanctioned by the Family. Mob law says you don't show respect at a funeral if the man dies on the Family's orders. Everything pointed to the murder being an outside job.

But what perplexed investigators the most was the fact that a mobster had turned up dead at all. In response to an internal war in the Colombo Family in the early nineties that left more than ten men dead, the FBI and the attorney general's office had turned up the heat on organized crime, bringing many of the city's rackets to a halt. New York's mob bosses knew it was the bodies that were attracting the attention, so they imposed a moratorium on murders. In fact, before Sciascia's murder, New York had seen just one other mobster rubbed out since the Colombo War ended in 1992. Now the Feds had the body of a known Mafia captain on their hands, and no clue what to make of it.

Assistant U.S. Attorney Robert Henoch presented the opening argument at Massino's 2004 trial. It was Mafia 101 for the jurors, complete with a big whiteboard showing the Bonanno Family tree. Massino lounged emotionless at the defense table with his attorney. The spectators in the gallery were silent. Henoch's partner, Greg Andres, the lead prosecutor, sat up straight at the prosecution table. Henoch shuffled his notes and took his position at the microphone.

HENOCH: "May it please the court, Mr. Breitbart, Mrs. Edwards [the defense lawyers], Mr. Massino, members of the jury, good morning. This trial is about the vicious, violent, cunning and murderous rise to power of Joseph Massino.

"Mr. Massino, the defendant seated between his attorneys, is the boss of the Bonanno Crime Family. The Bonanno Family makes its money through crime, arson, loan-sharking, gambling, extortion, racketeering and murder.

"The defendant has been involved in the Bonanno Crime Family since the mid-1970s. He has been running the Family since the 1980s. He's worked his way up in the Family from associate to soldier to captain. Now he sits as the boss of the Family, on top of a criminal organization that acts outside the laws of the United States and the laws of New York State.

"There are hundreds of made members in this family, and hundreds of associates. The Bonanno Crime Family uses all means necessary to earn its illegal profits, and any and all means necessary to protect its organization and its members. If you mess up on the job with the Bonanno Family, you don't get a bad report card, you don't get a negative performance evaluation, you don't get a slap on the wrist. Failure is not answered with criticism. Failure is punished by death.

"The defendant and his accomplices, over the course of this conspiracy, have conspired to murder and murdered seven different people. Victims of the murders— some were left in the streets, some were buried in shallow and unmarked graves, some were cut to pieces, others disappeared and were never heard from again.

"By way of background, let me talk for a moment about Cosa Nostra. Cosa Nostra is the Italian phrase for 'Our thing' or 'This thing of ours,' and it's also what is frequently referred to as the Mafia. In New York City, there are five Mafia Families, as the evidence will prove beyond a reasonable doubt: Lucchese, Colombo, Gambino, Genovese, Bonanno.

"Now, each one of those Families has a similar structure, each one of these Families has a similar set of rules that they go by. It's basically a secret organization of criminals. And some of those professional criminals are going to testify from that stand, and we're going to call them, and they are professional criminals that know the defendant, because they have been around him for twenty and thirty years.

"You're going to hear from those witnesses. You're going to hear all the different crimes those witnesses committed, and the different crimes that the defendant committed. You're going to hear about the legal and semilegal scams that they got involved in, as well—how they were involved in the stock market, the parking lot business, catering trucks, things like that.

"They are going to testify from that stand."

Salvatore Vitale didn't usually come to the Upper East Side. Like his brother-in-law, Joseph Massino, he was a Queens guy, complete with slicked-back hair, gold chains and an attitude to match. He looked out of place as he waited on a corner outside the fine wine store In Vino Veritas, famous among connoisseurs for being the first to open in Manhattan after Prohibition. But Vitale wasn't there to pick up a bottle of Pinot Grigio—he'd come to meet an alleged killer.

According to courtroom testimony, Bonanno captain Patrick "Patty from the Bronx" DeFilippo was staying at an apartment at Seventy-fourth Street and First Avenue. After a few minutes, DeFilippo squeezed through the front door of the building and popped out onto the street. He was a gorilla of a man. The two greeted each other, but didn't bother with small talk. "You know what we've got to do, Patty," said Vitale. DeFilippo nodded. "Do you need a car?" Vitale asked. DeFilippo said no. "Well," Vitale continued, "how are you going to do this? Explain it to me." DeFilippo assured him that he had it under control: Sciascia might balk at getting into a car he didn't recognize, so DeFilippo had decided to get a pickup truck belonging to one of his men, John "Johnny Joe" Spirito. Johnny Joe was well known among Bonannos, and DeFilippo knew Sciascia would recognize his white pickup. "Good," said Vitale. "Now," he went on, "I'll get the gun. I want you to dump the body in the street. Make it look like a drug deal gone wrong." Vitale didn't want to attract any cowboy vendettas from Sciascia's Montreal crew. "We don't want to get involved in a war," he added. There was one more question: how to lure Sciascia to the truck. DeFilippo explained that he and Sciascia recently had a business disagreement, and that Sciascia wouldn't be suspicious if he said he wanted to make amends. He would tell Sciascia to meet at Café 79, where he could talk him into having a private conversation in the pickup truck. At the right moment, he'd open fire.

The next day, Vitale drove to a quiet spot in Brooklyn. He got out and walked around to an alleyway behind a restaurant, where a car was parked in the shadows. He opened the passenger door and jumped in. Sitting in the driver's seat was Bonanno captain Anthony "Tony Green" Urso. Urso handed Vitale a brown paper bag, inside of which were two pistols: a .38 and a .25. The .25 was fitted with a silencer. After a brief exchange, Vitale got out and went back to his car with the bag tucked under his arm.

That evening he drove back to Manhattan. He parked his car on York Avenue and walked into a nearby steak house, where DeFilippo was sitting at a table. Vitale slid into the booth and under the table quietly passed him the bag containing the guns. After a few minutes of chitchat, they casually got up and walked outside to talk. "I want to test the gun," DeFilippo said. They hopped into a friend's car, which had a sunroof; as they drove around the block, DeFilippo pointed the gun at the sky and fired.

On the night of the Sciascia hit, Vitale drove into Manhattan in his son's SUV. He reached the Upper East Side by eight thirty. He still had another half hour before Sciascia was due to die, so he circled the neighborhood killing time, going over the plan in his mind. When it came to murder, Vitale didn't make mistakes: he'd had a lot of practice on his way to becoming an official underboss. In any other Family, his rank would have exempted him from the dirty jobs. But things had changed since Joe Massino had gotten out of prison— Vitale wasn't such a big shot now. And even though his sister Josephine was Massino's wife, Sal Vitale knew better than to complain. He tried to put his frustrations aside as he pulled up next to a pay phone on the corner of DeFilippo's apartment and dialed the captain's number.

"Patty, what's up?" said Vitale. DeFilippo knew better than to talk on the phone. He came down to the street and walked over to where Vitale was waiting. "It's done," said DeFilippo. "It's over." Without another word, DeFilippo passed him the .38 and walked back across the street. Vitale slipped another quarter into the phone and called Tony Green. They arranged to meet in the same spot as before. Vitale drove to Brooklyn, handed him the gun and left.

First thing the next morning, Vitale's beeper burst to life. It was DeFilippo—he needed to talk, urgently. They arranged to meet at a diner they knew off the Belt Parkway. When Vitale arrived, DeFilippo looked like he hadn't slept all night. He recounted how Johnny Joe had dumped the body as planned and gotten away clean—but there was a problem. "You got to get rid of the truck for me," said DeFilippo. "There's too much blood in it." Both men knew that, as Sciascia's mob associates, they'd immediately be under suspicion, and if the police found the truck they'd be finished. Vitale took the news in stride—with as many hits under his belt as he had, he knew how to handle a crisis. After saying good-bye to DeFilippo, he contacted a Bonanno soldier he'd used in similar jams. "I need to make a truck disappear as soon as possible," Vitale said. "No problem," replied the man, "where do you want to leave it so I can pick it up?" Vitale told him it would be at the corner of 159th and Crossbay Boulevard in Queens, and that the keys would be under the mat. "After you get done chopping the truck, bring me back the keys and the registration." He'd need them, he said, to do the insurance job.

David Breitbart had heard it all before. The Family! La Cosa Nostra! The Mafia! The veteran defense attorney sat quietly as the ambitious young prosecutor sprang about in front of a big white chart purporting to show the Bonanno Family Tree. Breitbart's record spoke for itself: most of the men he defended, many of them accused gangsters, walked free. He waited for Henoch to finish before taking his place on what he calls "my stage."

BREITBART: "Joe Massino has lived in New York all his life. He is sixty-one years of age. He has three beautiful kids. Two of them are sitting here in the front row, as his wife of forty-four years is sitting in the front row, totally devoted to him. He is a human being who is entitled to your attention, and entitled to the integrity of the system. He sits here presumed to be innocent. Without that, there's nowhere to go.

"Why are we here? Why Joseph Massino? They have their reasons. Joseph Massino had it tough. He even has a criminal record. Believe that or not, he does. He's been in trouble before. And as of June 25, 1991, the FBI has issued report after report after report indicating that he had ascended to the top rung of the Bonanno Family. Now, I don't say crime family. That's an appellation used by the federal government, 'crime family.' There's a difference, the Bonanno Family and the Bonanno Crime Family.

"The FBI believes he took over the role of leader of the Bonanno Family when a fellow by the name of Philip Rastelli died in 1991. So, for the last twelve years, the government alleges that he's been the boss.

"But that, in and of itself, is not the point.

"Whether or not Joe Massino is the boss is not sufficient evidence to prove him guilty of one of these charges. You can join a group, and it's no more guilt-bearing than the Knights of Columbus or the Boy Scouts of America.

"So what do you do? What do you do if you are a zealot and you want to make a case and you want to be the one to lock up the man they've been calling the Last Don? Well, how do you make such a case? How do you make such a case if there is no physical evidence? There are no fingerprints. There are no photographs. There is no resin. There are no scrapings.

"But they have a way: they call it a historical conspiracy case. They have to get somebody to say, 'The devil made me do it.' You get a few people who are in trouble in the world, who are facing life in prison or the death penalty, and you tell them, 'If you give us Joe Massino, you can go home.'

"There are witnesses [in this case] who were seduced by the government to testify against Joseph Massino. I know who they are. They have to tell us. How do you recruit a witness? Do you bribe them? Do they torture them? You better believe it."

GREG ANDRES: "Objection."

JUDGE GARAUFIS: "Overruled."

BREITBART: "I am going to prove to you that they use the same methods that were being used in Iraq—"

ANDRES: "Objection."

JUDGE GARAUFIS: "Overruled."

BREITBART: "That the same methods that were used in Iraq are being used at the Metropolitan Detention Center on Twenty-ninth Street in Brooklyn, and the MCC in Manhattan. People are taken from one cell to another and put on the ninth floor, and they are locked down 24/7, with the lights on, with the TV cameras going, so that they are sleep-deprived and weakened. And then, they are offered a deal.

"They are told by the United States Attorney, 'You don't have to go to jail for the rest of your life. You can join Team America. If you testify against Joe Massino, you can go home.' Ladies and gentlemen, that's what we are talking about here. We are talking about individuals who are going to be called to testify, who committed five, six, seven, eleven, twenty murders. Is that seduction? Is that bribery? Is that torture? I most respectfully suggest it is."

Salvatore Vitale liked Gerlando Sciascia, considered him a good man. They'd been partners in crime since the seventies. They went to weddings and wakes together, did hits together. In their thirty-year friendship, they'd killed four men together. All of that time, both had been fiercely loyal to Massino. When Massino was a captain, they were his closest lieutenants. As boss, Massino promoted them to the highest ranks within the Family.

But personal feelings meant nothing in the face of mob business. Massino gave Vitale a direct order to kill Sciascia. If he'd refused, he would have faced death himself, because as boss of the Family, Massino's word was law. He held the lives of everyone in his Family—more than one hundred made men—in his hands. If they questioned his authority or erred in any way, he'd crush them with a snap of his fleshy fingers. Sciascia made such a mistake in early 1999; he complained to Massino about Anthony Graziano, a Bonanno captain Massino happened to be fond of, saying he had a nasty cocaine habit. Old-fashioned gangsters like Sciascia thought drug use attracted too much attention. But in comparison to Graziano's indiscretion, Sciascia had made a far bigger blunder: he questioned Massino's authority. For a Mafia boss at the height of his power, there was only one course to be taken.

One night, shortly after Sciascia's throwaway comment, Massino sat alone with Sal Vitale at a table in the back of a dingy pizza restaurant behind JFK Airport. (The restaurant, D'Amici's, belonged to Vitale's niece and nephew, who that year celebrated their twenty-fifth wedding anniversary.) Using the background noise to muffle his voice, Massino leaned over to Vitale and whispered, "George has got to go." As he stood up to leave, Massino added that he and Josephine were leaving for a vacation in Cancun in the morning and would be gone a week. He cast Vitale another hard stare and left him with one last command.

"Get it done before I get home."

Without realizing it, Massino had just ordered the most serious crime of his career. Sure, he'd had more men killed than a Texas governor, but the hit on Sciascia, in the eyes of the law at least, was different, because in 1994, a Federal murder-in-aid-of-racketeering law was updated to include the death sentence. Whacking Sciascia had just put Massino in the same league as Murder Inc.'s Louis "Lepke" Buchalter, who was electrocuted in 1944. If Massino was caught and convicted for the Sciascia hit, he could have become the first American mobster to be executed in a generation.

TWO

SOMEPLACE IN QUEENS

Before the implosion, the Maspeth gas holders poked skyward four hundred feet, rising out of a crumbled industrial zone on the Queens-Brooklyn border. The twin steel giants held the methane required to maintain the proper pressure in residential gas lines. They were a tepid shade of brown, although their upper rims were painted red and white in a three-layered checkered pattern—a color scheme designed to ward off low-flying aircraft. Had a plane ever failed to notice the tanks, the surrounding area would have been scorched flat in a millisecond.

The holders were a major landmark for the people of Maspeth. Built in 1927 and 1948, respectively, the giants were reputed to have occupied the spot where Buffalo Bill Cody once kept a corral of horses for his traveling Wild West Show. Local folk would describe their neighborhood by saying it was "near the tanks." So when they tumbled in a spectacular double demolition in July 2001, the Maspeth residents felt a distinct sense of loss. A hole was left in the sky; a piece of their identity, albeit an utterly hideous one, had collapsed in a great cloud of lead dust. The community's mourning was so great that a yearlong public art display was erected in honor of the holders: ten gray metal shoebox-shaped containers were bolted to the rivet-studded walkway over the Pulaski Bridge, the fifty-year-old drawbridge spanning the contaminated Newton Creek near where the holders had stood. Each box had a window revealing a photographic transparency of the holders' last moments, shown in sequence from the instant of detonation to oblivion. If you walked across the bride glancing at each transparency, you witnessed an animated replay of the implosion. The display was titled *Premonition,* because the demolition took place just two months before September 11, 2001.

* * *

It's said that if you polled New Yorkers about which of the five boroughs they know best, Queens would rank near the bottom, above only Staten Island. If that's true, then Maspeth is to Queens what Queens is to New York—even the borough natives don't know where it is. Located on Queens's western frontier, to the east of the better-known Brooklyn localities of Greenpoint and Williamsburg, Maspeth is a largely forgotten town, particularly after losing its signature twin towers. Without the gas giants, the town is hidden behind both natural and man-made barriers: the foul blackness of Newton Creek and the concrete canyon of the Long Island Expressway. It is also surrounded by a ring of cemeteries where New York's dead have been deposited since the 1850s, when burials were banned in overcrowded Manhattan. Just about the only outsiders who do go to Maspeth, it seems, are truck drivers. The neighborhood's industrial lowlands, positioned alongside the Expressway, are a major trucking hub.

But the truth is, Maspeth folk like being forgotten. They don't mind being isolated and, in large part, overlooked by the rest of New York. In fact, the blue-collar natives, composed of primarily Italian and Polish immigrants, don't think of themselves as city dwellers at all. They call Maspeth a "town" not a neighborhood. The main street, Grand Avenue, boasts an American Legion post, Civil War–era buildings, wooden shingles, and hair salons with forty-year-old Formica interiors. A large sign on the corner of Grand Avenue and Sixty-ninth Street welcomes newcomers and proudly states that the town was founded in 1642, making Maspeth the oldest neighborhood in Queens. For generations, residents have made their homes on the same block in Maspeth. People stick together, and know what it means to live like family.

In the late 1970s, a business called J&S Cake was located on Fifty-eighth Road, Maspeth, at the bottom of the hill where the residential portion of the neighborhood meets the bowels of its industrial section. The club was around the corner from where a rusty Long Island Railroad bridge straddles Grand Avenue, located in the middle of a dead-quiet semi-industrial block. It had a tiny storefront sheathed in an intricate layer of stone masonry. Into that stone front were cut two small square windows that made the building look like a jailhouse. There were a few houses nearby, but mostly there were warehouses.

Everyone and no one knew about J&S Cake. Locals would refer to it with a knowing wink. Though it appeared to be just a plain two-story building, J&S Cake and the purpose it served were not camouflaged from the law-abiding citizens of Maspeth, nor the FBI. They knew it wasn't a bakery. In fact, they knew there wasn't a cake to be found there.

J&S Cake was the headquarters of a Mafia crew.

Behind the stone walls and the darkened front windows, which allowed you to see out but not in, was a dimly lit, rudimentary front room, roughly thirty by twenty feet. It was worn and scuffed, and featured a bar, a coffee machine and a card table. In that room, the most powerful Bonanno in Queens was king. Joe Massino, known to his men as "Joe the Chief," ran a big business out of little J&S Cake, and his trade was crime. He controlled the neighborhood numbers and sports betting rackets. His men lent money on the street, and made a killing fencing stolen goods and hijacking trucks. But it wasn't just about money: in the seventies, when

City Hall couldn't afford to pick up the garbage and muggers prowled the subways, Massino was a well-known figure on the working-class streets of Maspeth. He made himself available to those who needed a favor. Local people came to ask for help to start a business or just pay a bill. "He helped me get custody of my daughter," recalled one local resident. His illegal gambling rackets employed Maspeth residents, and thanks to him, a few players got lucky. Except for Sundays, which he spent with his family, Massino's door was always open. Every other day of the week, his coarse lieutenants rolled around J&S Cake like empty beer bottles. They included James "Big Louie" Tartaglione, a loan shark and arsonist; Duane "Goldie" Leisenheimer, a car thief and wheelman; Raymond "Ray" Wean, a card dealer, truck driver and enforcer; and most important, Salvatore "Good-Looking Sal" Vitale, Massino's second in charge, chief hitman and fellow J&S Cake namesake (the "J" stood for Joey, the "S" for Sal).

Tuesday was the big night at the club. Gangsters from around the city came to pay their respects, talk sports and trade coarse laughs. It was an opportunity for the guys to meet up and see the Chief. They ate, drank and played cards—Massino's game of choice was continental (a form of gin rummy played with four decks and a joker for each player). The stakes would reach into the thousands by the night's end. The players had nicknames including Dirty Danny, Big Willie, Patty Muscles, Peter Rabbit, TG, Cheech, Joe C, Mickey Batts, Shellackhead, Lefty Guns, Joe Shakes and Louie HaHa.

The more they came, the more powerful Massino became. Being connected to Massino gave them clout; in return, the chief found strength in their numbers. He was their protection on the street. And they were his private army.

Duane Leisenheimer stood out from the Italian kids in Maspeth. His full head of blond hair and his bright blue eyes turned heads in the neighborhood, where his nickname had been Goldie for as long as he could remember. He didn't have much time for grade school—early on, Goldie had picked up a love for anything mechanical from his engineer father. He spent long summer afternoons tinkering with his bicycle. He was obsessed with cars long before he was legally able to drive—he knew the specs of every new model Buick or Oldsmobile by heart. In the early seventies, when he was still in elementary school, he got a job in a local garage. After school, he'd go in to sweep up, pick up tools and do coffee runs for the mechanics. Soon he was doing minor repair jobs himself, fixing sticky windows and replacing old radiator hoses. While he was there, he got to know the men from the neighborhood, street guys who'd bring in their cars for repairs. Two of his acquaintances he knew only as "Rusty" and "Joey." It wasn't until several years later that he learned they were in fact the infamous gangsters Phil Rastelli and Joey Massino.

Goldie stole his first car when he was sixteen—a '67 Chevy. It was a lot more fun than sweeping floors. He'd dropped out of high school (Brooklyn Automotive) after only one year. By seventeen, he was working in a chop shop run by a local criminal. A professional car thief, he taught Goldie a lot more than school ever did. They'd rip apart cars and sell the parts to junkyards. By the time he was eighteen, Goldie was stealing cars full-time. When an order came in for either parts or a whole delivery, he and his mentor would drive around Queens until they found the car they needed. They'd use a screwdriver or a slap hammer to rip out the ignition and start it up. Goldie could steal up to fifteen cars a week and get paid $100 to $150 a pop, even more for a special order.

Goldie got to know Joey Massino personally in the early seventies. He lived in the neighborhood, and every morning he'd see Massino filling up his catering truck. The chop shop guy was also pals with Massino, and Goldie would tag along when he stopped in to see Joe. He assured Massino that Goldie was a stand-up guy despite his obviously non-Italian roots—no way would he rat if he got pinched.

The kid loved the big man right from the start. Massino let him help with his catering truck, and even recruited him to steal cars to take out on scores. But the boss cautioned Goldie not to steal any from the neighborhood. He once berated him for parking a stolen car on the same block as his store. "I don't want your heat and you don't want mine," Massino warned. He also tipped him off to the areas around town to avoid. Massino's friend John Gotti, then a Gambino soldier, hung out at the Cozy Corner Bar on Grand Avenue, only a mile up the hill from Massino's store. It was a gambling den. In 1982, a man was shot nine times inside the club but lived. "I hope you're not stealing cars over by that club," Massino told Goldie. "If those guys catch you, you're going to wind up in the trunk of a car."

Massino schooled Goldie in the art of countersurveillance. Like any good wiseguy, the chief was paranoid— he always assumed he was being watched by law enforcement. He'd drill the impressionable youngster before he sent him out to steal a car or drive a stolen truck. "Be careful. Watch your mirrors. Make sure no one is following you." And Goldie had good reason to heed Massino's advice. One day, he arrived at the store just as Sal Vitale was getting ready to head over to a warehouse to help unload a stolen truck. But something didn't feel right. "That van doesn't belong here," Massino said, pointing at a vehicle parked outside. He knew every car in the neighborhood, and that one didn't fit. Vitale was getting antsy—he knew guys were waiting with the stolen rig—so he left. But as soon as he did, the van pulled out after him. Massino and Goldie scrambled into a car, sped ahead to the warehouse and rushed inside, yelling for everyone to scram. When FBI stormed in minutes later they found the building deserted.

Another time, Massino and Goldie were standing on the sidewalk outside J&S Cake. The chief inconspicuously raised his eyes upward. "Look up there," he said. Goldie glanced up and saw a rectangular box fixed to the roof. He was staring straight into the barrel of a camera. Massino thought it best to pretend they never knew—he wanted to let the Feds think they were getting something. But eventually, curiosity got the better of Goldie. One afternoon, he and Sal Vitale carried a ladder to the end of the street and hoisted themselves up on the building with the camera. The wooden box was about the size of a stereo speaker; a hole had been cut in one of the ends and was neatly covered with a piece of glass. The camera inside was recording the busy ants below. The two men joked about throwing the box off the roof. "I don't think the Chief would like that," reconsidered Vitale. Pull a stunt like that, they agreed, and Massino would be even more pissed than the FBI.

Massino would recruit Goldie when stolen trucks were brought into the neighborhood. The first time he did was when the men needed help unpacking a load of Huckapoo shirts (floral shirts that were fashionable in the seventies). When he arrived at the drop point, Goldie saw Massino and his men were having problems: the truck had an alarm, and they couldn't get into the trailer without setting it off. Goldie used an acetylene torch to cut the alarm box off the side of the truck. He then used a screwdriver to deactivate it. Massino quickly learned that Goldie was a handy kid to have around, and would pay him roughly two thousand dollars for a half hour's work.

Goldie was never officially initiated into the mob because he wasn't Italian. Nevertheless, he was a full-time Bonanno associate by his twentieth birthday. He was a fixture at Massino's club and one of his most trusted men.

More than thirty years later, at Massino's 2004 trial, Duane "Goldie" Leisenheimer took his seat in the witness box to testify against his former mentor. That he'd been a mobster seemed almost impossible—he was lanky and blond, more California surfer than New York greaseball. His fine, strawlike hair was parted down the center and hung low down over his ears. He was forty-seven years old, and had been happily married for fourteen years. He hadn't stolen a car in more than a decade. But in 2003, when his wife opened the door to two FBI agents, his past suddenly caught up with him.

HENOCH: "How would Mr. Massino refer to cars that didn't belong on the block?"

LEISENHEIMER: "They were referred to as 'bad cars.' "

HENOCH: "When you saw a car you believed to be bad, would you tell anyone?"

LEISENHEIMER: "Yes. I would make it my business to go stop by and tell whoever was around there was a bad car in the neighborhood."

HENOCH: "Did you become familiar with the sort of vehicles that law enforcement used around the club?"

LEISENHEIMER: "Yeah."

HENOCH: "And can you tell the jury what sort of vehicles were used?"

LEISENHEIMER: "A white van, a blue Ford van, a '79 Chevy Malibu, a Ford Topaz, I think. Had quite a few of them."

HENOCH: "How did you learn those cars were being used by law enforcement?"

LEISENHEIMER: "They were around so much you knew what they were—that they were bad cars."

HENOCH: "Was there something called the Clinton Diner anywhere nearby?"

LEISENHEIMER: "Yes."

HENOCH: "Did you ever make any observation at the Clinton Diner with respect to the FBI and the police cars and bad cars?"

LEISENHEIMER: "Yes. They used to park their cars along the back of the Clinton Diner and switch. They used to park three or four of them in there, jump in one and drive off. I assume when we made the car or something, they would change and get in another one."

Maspeth, Queens, was Bonanno Family territory long before Massino took over. Rusty Rastelli was also a Maspeth native. Like his successor, he was a hardened street thug: an extortionist, loan shark and labor racketeer (his first run-in with the law occurred at the tender age of eight). He ran a social club nestled among a handful of shops at the bottom end of Grand Avenue— a white, three-story wooden building, with a storefront and apartments above, just around the corner from where Massino would later open J&S Cake.

In 1966, Rastelli established an organization called the Workmen's Mobile Lunch Association. Lunch truck drivers who joined the association were charged "dues" of ten to fifteen dollars a week in return for a guarantee they'd wouldn't face competition anywhere in Brooklyn, Queens and Nassau County. One non-association driver who ventured onto Rastelli's turf was beaten up; another had his truck smashed in. Rastelli's men shook down food wholesalers, telling them Association members would boycott their goods if they didn't cough up. One wholesaler said he paid five hundred dollars a month to the Family. But the picnic didn't last forever: in 1975, Rastelli was busted for the extortion scheme and sentenced to ten years in prison.

After Rastelli was jailed, Massino remained fiercely loyal to him. Joe once said, "He is like my uncle, he raised me, baptized me. I can't abandon him." But by that point, Massino was well on his way to filling Rastelli's shoes. He had already opened his own storefront deli, J&J Catering, located on 58th Road, Maspeth. (Massino opened J&S Cake about a decade after he opened J&J. In fact, Cake was located right behind it, so close their backyards were touching.) The deli was a perfect front for his early criminal rackets. His wife, Josephine, helped him run the business, which was named after the young couple—one J for Joey and one for Josephine. She was a striking, petite young woman with fine facial features and long dark hair. Born in Sicily, Josephine immigrated with her family to the United States when she was a child and settled in Bushwick, Brooklyn. Her younger brother, Sal Vitale, was born in America. She married Joe Massino in 1960, and the two settled in Maspeth. In the early seventies, they lived happily with their three young daughters in a modest redbrick home on Caldwell Avenue, about a mile from the deli. The house had a knee-high front gate made of metal, with the letters "JM" blended into the ironwork. At the corners of the gate, on brick posts, stood two little statues of lions, painted white. They were anything but quaint. In Italian culture, lions signify strength.

Just as Phil Rastelli had done, Massino ran a fleet of catering trucks, which he filled up with coffee and cakes to be sold. He drove one himself and every morning would set off on his allocated route, making stops at factories and truck terminals in industrial Queens. As Massino handed the workers their morning cup of joe, they handed him merchandise stolen from the rigs' trailers. They brazenly snatched anything of value left sitting on the loading platforms and piled it into the wagon; Massino simply drove away and sold the goods. When he returned the next time, he would give the workers a third of the wholesale value of whatever he unloaded. One of Massino's main suppliers was a hulking driver and yard switcher named Ray Wean (who later joined Massino's J&S Cake hijacking crew). Wean once slipped Massino a huge load of electrical appliances; another time he gave him Kodak cameras. Their biggest score was three hundred cases of valuable flash bulbs.

Massino eventually put together his own fleet of roughly twenty wagons, supplying them with food from his deli, J&J Catering. Always working an angle, he had his drivers double as numbers runners. Numbers betting is the New York Mafia's very own lottery, and continues to be a way of life in working-class neighborhoods across the city. Players select numbers between zero and 999. The winning number, or "Brooklyn number," is derived from horse racing: it is the last three digits before the decimal point of the "total mutual handle," the amount of money bet in a day at a particular racetrack. Every day, a committee representing each of the Five Families makes a joint decision as to which racetrack will provide the day's number. Players check to see if they've won by consulting the *New*

York Post or *Daily News* racing pages. The odds of winning the illegal lottery are 999 to 1. Winners are paid either 600 or 500 to 1, depending on the racket, giving the racketeer a clear advantage.

When Massino's drivers would return from their runs, they'd tell Massino how many hits they had on their sheets. He'd take the earnings, pay the drivers their cut and give them whatever they needed to pay the winners when they went out on their next runs. The system was brilliant. Massino's trucks allowed him unparalleled access to the factories and warehouses of Maspeth, where numbers betting was as common as bad coffee and bagels. They made him a lynchpin of New York's illegal gambling community.

Good-Looking Sal Vitale, Massino's second in command, ran the Family's other gambling racket, sports betting, which offered people the chance to bet on professional sports including baseball, basketball and football. The phones rang hot all day every day in the bookie's "wire room," which was strewn with messy desks and rotary phones (and was often set up in a makeshift temporary apartment that could be packed up and abandoned as soon as the heat was on). A blackboard gave the "current line" on games and the odds jibed with those given in Las Vegas—the only place in America where sports betting is legal.

Sal had two "controllers," one known as "Max" and the other as "Black," who were paid five hundred dollars a week. Each one kept a sheet of bets and personally kept tabs on their bettors, only established neighborhood customers whom they knew they could trust. Each customer was assigned an identification number; to place a bet, he would call the wire room, state his number, distinguish which controller he wanted to bet with and make his wager. Most of the time, bettors placed a straight wager on a team to win, but football and basketball had a spread. In other words, Vitale gave the favorite a points advantage: if he had the Giants down as a five-point favorite over the Eagles, the Giants had to win by at least five to pay. Vitale also charged a commission or "vig" on losing bets, ten cents on the dollar. Each week, Vitale would tell Massino whether or not they had made money by saying they had a "red" or a "blue" figure. If it was blue, they were ahead, and Vitale would give half the takings to Massino. If they found themselves a long way ahead, they might even stop taking bets to hedge against a possible loss.

Unlike legitimate sports betting, Vitale gave gamblers credit whenever they needed it, which allowed them to wager huge amounts of money with a simple phone call. He would set the amount of credit for each customer based on his reputation for paying. At the end of the week, "runners" would be sent out to settle up. The operation was small compared to New York's bigger sports bookies, which might have had as many as fifty controllers running bets. On a good week, Massino and Vitale might have turned a twelve-thousand-dollar profit. But it was a piece of the puzzle—a small part of the formidable organized crime enterprise Massino was building from within the unforgiving limits of Maspeth, Queens.

The numbers and sports games were good businesses, to be sure. But in the 1970s, truck hijacking was by far Joe Massino's most lucrative racket. It's easy to see why: he was operating beside one of the biggest trucking hubs on the East Coast. Hundreds of interstate rigs traveled back and forth through Maspeth every day, grinding into the isolated neighborhood over the single-lane bridge spanning Newton Creek and traveling right past Massino's headquarters. On one occasion,

Massino got a tip-off that a truckload of frozen shrimp was going to be coming by. It was a thirty-thousand-dollar score, and he had a buyer all lined up. His crew waited outside of the warehouse in Queens where they knew the truck would emerge. As the rig pulled out, two of Massino's men T-boned a stolen van into its side. They grabbed the driver and his passenger, threw them in the van and sped away. Another crewman hopped into the truck and took off. "We took the guy right out of the truck, right in broad daylight," Sal Vitale would later brag.

It was that kind of job that earned Massino a reputation as one of New York's most prolific hijackers. The racket was big business in the seventies: a load of pharmaceuticals, imported suits or lobster tails could bring in hundreds of thousands of dollars. At the time, up to ten trucks were being jacked every week in Queens and Brooklyn, costing merchants roughly three hundred thousand dollars a day. Stolen trucks were driven to a prearranged "drop" and quickly unloaded before being driven away and abandoned. The goods were fenced to neighborhood traders, even supermarkets, below the wholesale price. In many cases, the heists were "give-ups." The drivers knew in advance they were going to be hijacked and simply stopped the truck and handed it over. As the racket spun out of control, the FBI and NYPD worked around the clock trying to foil the hijackers. The cops were so desperate they resorted to patrolling above highways in helicopters using night vision equipment.

Along with Massino, New York's other major hijackers were John Gotti and Brooklyn Bonanno captain Dominick "Sonny Black" Napolitano. The three were close associates: they bought and sold each other's swag (stolen goods) and provided drops when one or the other brought in a fresh load. Massino once bought two hundred cases of Chicken of the Sea tuna from Sonny Black to use to make sandwiches in his deli. "I had to be crazy when I bought two hundred cases of tuna fish off Sonny," laughed Massino, according to an informant. Massino became so deeply involved in the trucking game, he even had his own truck "consulting" company: MVP Trucking, which was listed at the same address as J&S Cake. Of course, Massino didn't know the first thing about trucks—except how to hijack them.

Inevitably, Massino and his hijacking crew had a few close scrapes with the law. On one occasion, his crew had gotten hold of a load of sneakers. Gordon McEwan, an NYPD detective, had taken a 4 a.m. call from an informant alerting him to the heist. He met the informant in an industrial area behind Shea Stadium in Queens. Beyond a metal fence, the detective spied a truck trailer parked in a yard; before long, another truck pulled into the yard. A "heavyset man," who the cops later identified as Massino, was directing that vehicle. At 12:30 p.m. Detective McEwan made a pass in his car. "I observed a paint roller on the long pole going up and down the side of one of the trailers," he later testified, "and someone was painting over the PCL (identification) numbers with silver paint." Just over an hour later the detective and FBI agents burst onto the scene, but Massino was gone. "I found in the back of the yard a piece of corrugated metal that could be moved so a person could fit in and out of the fence," McEwan said. The detective discovered hundreds of cartons of Mitsubishi-branded sneakers. They'd been stolen from a warehouse in New Jersey, and were valued at two hundred thousand dollars.

Sometimes, Massino came face-to-face with the men trying to put him behind bars, as he did during one memorable heist in 1975. Ray Wean spotted an idle truck in downtown Manhattan, parked at a curb. Wean, who had the physique of a small building, saw household goods inside, which he assumed were valuable. He leapt in, started the truck and sped to Maspeth, where he arranged to meet Massino at the Clinton Diner, not far from J&J Catering.

FBI agent Pat Colgan was on duty in Queens that day. Colgan was a burly agent in the Theft from Interstate Trucking Squad, who kept close tabs on Massino. Within an hour of the truck going missing, Colgan's supervisor contacted him and told him to be on the lookout. Colgan jumped into his unmarked Plymouth and sped to Massino's neighborhood. His hunch was right—there he spotted a small truck parked near the Clinton Diner that matched the description he had been given. From his vantage point, he observed career criminal Wean climb into the cabin and drive away. Colgan gunned his engine and squealed after the truck. Suddenly, Massino, who was driving a blue Cadillac, flashed past. "Our eyes met," Colgan later testified. "He proceeded to continue behind the tractor trailer. The tractor trailer stopped for a traffic light and Mr. Massino pulled up alongside." Wean was oblivious until he saw his boss. "Joe Massino pulled up alongside and screamed that the FBI was behind him, to get rid of the truck." Colgan followed the truck for another quarter mile. Then, Wean stopped, jumped down and began to wander away as if nothing was wrong. Colgan quickly arrested him. "Wean is so goddamn big," Colgan recalled in an interview, "I couldn't get the cuffs on him."

Massino got out of his car just as Colgan was stuffing Wean into his vehicle. "Hey, what are you doing?" he yelled. Colgan replied, "I'm arresting your buddy and by the way, you're under arrest too. Get your ass over here." Massino bought himself some time by appealing to Colgan's sympathy: he asked if he could go to the toilet. "Fine," said Colgan. "Use the bathroom in the restaurant, come back and we'll talk."

"He immediately returned to his vehicle," Colgan recalled, "made a U-turn and proceeded to give me a finger gesture as he sped away." The agent, who had his hands full with an unshackled prisoner, could only watch helplessly as his primary target escaped. But his frustration was short-lived—Massino returned a half hour later to the site of the altercation, and turned himself in. Later, in a jail cell, the Bonanno boss was furious. He spent his days trying not to be caught, and now he had gotten caught for this? As it turned out, the truck's contents were valued at just ten thousand dollars. Wean had brought him a "garbage load." (The police couldn't get the charges to stick, and Massino was later released.)

Good-Looking Sal had a habit of searching for electronic bugs in J&S Cake. At least once a week, he'd get up on a ladder to search the ceiling, or look under the furniture. One day, he found something hidden above the card table. Less than twenty-four hours before, a team of FBI agents (led by newly promoted supervisor Colgan) had been inside J&S Cake. Armed with a Title 3 warrant, more than forty agents installed an "RF" (radio frequency) bug in the ceiling before slipping away into the night. For a few short hours the next day, Radio Massino came in loud and clear. Colgan had a glimpse of what had eluded him for so many years: hard evidence against Massino. Then, suddenly, the bug went dead.

Little did Colgan know, that was far from the end of the story. Back at FBI headquarters the next day, he got called into a meeting. "Pat," said an unsympathetic superior, "you've got to get the equipment back." The bugging device was extremely expensive and in short supply. Colgan was stunned. "What do you want me to do?" he asked. "I don't care what you do," his boss snapped back. "You know Massino. Go ask him if you can go up in the ceiling and get it."

Colgan swallowed his pride and drove out to J&S Cake. He paused for a few minutes outside, trying to decide what to do. He just couldn't knock on the door of a Mafia club, could he? Just then, a car pulled up. Sal Vitale got out, walked to the door and put his key in the lock. Colgan saw his opportunity. He briskly walked up behind Vitale, and, just as Sal stepped inside, he coattailed in behind him. "Who are you?" Vitale demanded as he swung around. "I'm looking for Joey," Colgan said bluntly. Vitale threw a wild punch but missed. Colgan, the bigger of the two, pushed him down. "I told you, I'm looking for Joey."

Colgan's eyes were still adjusting to the dim light when he saw two or three men coming toward him. He thought his time was up. But suddenly he heard a voice call out, "Relax everybody, it's only Pat." It was Massino. "Hi Pat, how are you?" the Chief asked. Now able to see properly, Colgan returned the pleasantry.

Massino said, "I figured you'd be back." "Yeah, you were right," Colgan admitted, "I'd like to have our equipment back." The Chief rose from his chair, went to the back of the club, picked up a metal box, walked back past half a dozen wiseguys and put it down on the bar. "You want a beer?" he asked. Colgan replied that he'd like to, but he was on duty. "Don't worry," said Massino, "I'm buying."

The occasional friendly contact didn't diminish the magnitude of the battle between the two men. "It was a war, and there was a professional respect for your adversary," Colgan said in an interview of the man he pursued for fourteen of his twenty-eight years in the FBI. "But if it had been my life or his, hah, good-bye. We would have both been shooting and only one of us would have walked away. Joey didn't get the reputation he had on the street because he was Mr. Nice Guy. He was lethal," Colgan continued. "If he even thought you were an informant, he'd have you killed. If Joey said something, you did it. Didn't question why. People jumped. They wanted to be endeared to Joey. If they didn't do what he said, he'd whack them."

* * *

Goldie was an affable witness. The jurors tried hard not to smile at his worker's charm, especially at his obvious affection for automobiles. But nobody laughed when he testified as to just how dangerous Massino was. The car thief's former mentor, Joey Massino, sat stone-faced on the other side of the room.

HENOCH: "Was there ever a time in your life when you used illegal narcotics?"

LEISENHEIMER: "Yes."

HENOCH: "About what time was that?"

LEISENHEIMER: "Late seventies."

HENOCH: "Did you ever commit any crimes or steal cars or anything like that when you were using cocaine?"

LEISENHEIMER: "No."

HENOCH: "Why not?"

LEISENHEIMER: "Your guard was down. You never did anything when you were high or drunk."

HENOCH: "Did there come a time when you were involved in selling cocaine as well?"

LEISENHEIMER: "Yes."

HENOCH: "About how much money would you approximate you made from that?"

LEISENHEIMER: "Not much. Ten, fifteen thousand dollars, if I made that."

HENOCH: "And did there come a time that Mr. Massino had a conversation with you about selling drugs?"

LEISENHEIMER: "Oh, yeah."

HENOCH: "Can you tell the jury about that?"

LEISENHEIMER: "Mr. Massino told me, he says, 'Someone told me that you are involved in drug dealing and you know where I stand with that.' I say, 'Yeah.' He says, 'Well, I'm not going to tell you what to do, but you know I don't go for that and if you come around me and you are doing that, you are going to get hurt.' "

HENOCH: "And when he said you're going to get hurt, what did you take that to mean?"

LEISENHEIMER: "I would have been in trouble. If I would have gone around by him doing that, caused him any kind of trouble, he would have definitely killed me."

THREE

THE THREE CAPTAINS

The vacant lot was small and nondescript. The ground was soggy, and thanks to the night's rain, pools of putrid water had formed along the lot's street frontage. Nevertheless, to the inquisitive kids of Ozone Park, Queens, it looked like a good place to play. They enjoyed running through the tall weeds, and stopped now and then to pick through discarded junk.

That Sunday afternoon in late May 1981, the children followed a foul stench. The smell was coming from a roll of soiled bedclothes that were partly buried in a shallow ditch. One of the kids kicked at the find, inadvertently ending the group's little adventure: a layer of the sheet parted to reveal the cocked arm of a dead man, stiff and partly decomposed. Etched on the forearm was a faded tattoo depicting a dagger embedded in twin hearts—the classic design of the Sacred Heart, often associated with heartbreak. The children darted off in the direction of their respective parents. There would be no more games allowed that day.

Later, the medical examiner would note that the body was lying on its right side. It had been wrapped in a white bedsheet and had a length of cord wound tightly around the neck, torso and ankles. The deceased was dressed in an orange T-shirt, beige pants and brown cowboy boots. His Cartier watch had stopped at 5:58 on May 7th. The autopsy would show that he had been shot three times: one bullet traveled through his left ear and out the bottom of his right cheek. A second pierced the left side of his chest, passing through his body and out the right side of his back without entering his rib cage. The third bullet struck him in the small of the back. A lead .38-caliber projectile was found inside the man's shirt—the force of being fired into the body had flattened one of its ends on a sharp diagonal. The medical examiner concluded that the man had died from the gunshot wounds and internal hemorrhaging, and ruled the case a homicide.

The dead man was Alphonse "Sonny Red" Indelicato, a powerful captain in the Bonanno Family. He was identified when his decomposing fingertips were matched with print records. At the time of his murder, Sonny Red, fifty-four, was being investigated for his suspected role in the slaying of mob chieftan Joseph "Joe Crazy" Gallo, who had been rubbed out in Umberto's Clam House nine years earlier. Sonny Red was also a reputed narcotics trafficker and loan shark. Only a month before his death, FBI agents had photographed him walking with his son Bruno, also a Bonanno captain, in Long Island. The two were spotted strolling near the beach. Sonny Red wore only bright red Speedos—he was proud of his broad shoulders and sculptured torso.

Sonny Red's murder was the culmination of a vicious power struggle within the Family after the murder of Carmine Galante in 1979. At the time, Rusty Rastelli, already weakened by Galante's brief return to power, was still in prison, and the Bonannos lacked a visible leader. Three power-hungry factions emerged. One group led by Joe Massino and Sonny Black, the truck hijacker from Brooklyn, was still loyal to the imprisoned leader. Another, led by the three captains

Sonny Red, Philip "Phil Lucky" Giaccone and Dominick "Big Trin" Trinchera, no longer were. Sonny Red represented the Manhattan tentacle of the family, while Big Trin was from the Bronx. Phil Lucky had been Massino's captain in the seventies, but the two men had always disliked each other. The third faction was the Zips, the Sicilian wing of the Family (who got their nickname because American gangsters thought they spoke Italian so fast).

The Bonanno captains met in the months after the Galante murder to work out their differences. However, tension continued to grow, and eventually the dispute was taken to the Commission. It ruled there was to be no "gunplay." The captains were to make amends.

Sonny Red, Phil Lucky and Big Trin, the three members of the "Red Team" disappeared in May 1981. Sonny Red's rancid corpse surfaced a mere three weeks later, but it would be more than twenty years until the remains of the other two captains were discovered—buried just feet from where the children found Sonny Red. The storied hit, which was depicted in the film *Donnie Brasco,* would eventually become known as "the murder of the three captains."

* * *

Frank Lino didn't look like a wiseguy—in fact, he didn't even look Italian. He had curly, ginger hair, a round face and cherub cheeks with a ruddy complexion. His smile was toothy and his droopy eyes were set slightly too close together. It seemed the older he got, the more he inflated. But despite his unlikely appearance, Lino was born to be a gangster. Organized crime was in his blood: his parents were from Sicily, and just about every male in his family was in the mob. Lino's cousin Eddie was attached to the Gambino Family; his other cousin Bobby was a Bonanno. Lino had two sons of his own, one of whom, Joseph Lino, was a made man. During his forty-year criminal career in the mob, Lino was associated with four of the Five Families. He joined the Genoveses in 1956, switched to the Colombos in 1962 and went to the Gambinos in 1969. In 1977, his lifelong friend, Frank Coppa, helped him join the Bonannos. At the time, Carmine Galante was the power, and the family was hiring.

More than anything, Frank Lino was from Brooklyn—a real neighborhood wiseguy. After dropping out of high school in the fifties he joined a gang called the Avenue U Boys in the Bensonhurst section, which at the time was home to a flood of new immigrants from Sicily. The Avenue U Boys did robberies and rumbled with other gangs with names like the Zippers, the Ghosts, the Dandies, the Senators and the Silver Aces. Lino first became associated with the mob when he was seventeen, running card games for a local Genovese soldier. In 1962, he was arrested for the murders of two Brooklyn detectives. The detectives, aged twenty-eight and fifty-six, were shot dead during a holdup at a tobacco shop, where the robbers took five thousand dollars. Lino was charged after he supplied a car to get one of the gunmen to Chicago, and was one of five men charged after being taken to the 66th Precinct for "questioning." Lino later claimed the cops drove staples into his hands and a broomstick up his ass. He was left with a broken leg and broken arm. He was let off with three years' probation after he threatened to sue.

The mob life defined Frankie Lino. Crime was more than his job—it was all he knew. He'd done everything from selling "French films" to running pump-and-dump schemes on Wall Street. He was a loan shark, a bookie, a drug dealer and a killer—he took part in the murders of six men. Once he came back to his New York apartment after being in Pennsylvania and found it covered in blood. His cousin Eddie, who shared the place with him, explained there'd been an argument— something about ten thousand dollars, cocaine and a friend's wife. The party had ended in gunfire, and now there were two bodies in the trunk of a car outside, which they later buried near JFK. Lino had the place renovated from the floorboards up. It was the only way to get rid of the bloodstains.

Lino's one legitimate business was a bus company he started with his son in the late seventies, after winning a contract from the New York City Board of Education. Lino hardly knew the front end of a bus from the back, but he was listed as an "advisor" on the company tax records. Of course, he was doing a lot better than what he told the IRS: by the late nineties, as a captain, he was taking home more than two hundred thousand dollars. But he never saved a dime. Between his five children and twelve grandchildren, and his own lavish lifestyle— tailored suits, fancy restaurants, nightclubs and long trips abroad—he'd often close out the year at least $50,000 in debt. But somehow, Lino always managed to come out on top.

* * *

Lino sat hunched in the witness box at Massino's trial. Gone were the curls and the cheeky grin. At sixty-six years old, his face was pale and gaunt, his hair white. One of his eyes blinked uncontrollably—a legacy from the 1962 beating at the hands of the Brooklyn police. He was taking five types of medication for ailments ranging from high blood pressure to heart disease. After being subjected to solitary confinement for eighty-one days, Lino broke down and spilled his life story. For three days on the stand, he detailed his crimes for the attorneys and the jury, speaking with pride and a hint of melancholy. He'd been a Bonanno for twenty-seven years. His induction ceremony into the Family, he recalled, was on his thirty-ninth birthday: October 30, 1977. The ultra secret ritual was virtually the same as it had been at the turn of the century. His was conducted on Elizabeth Street, Little Italy—in Sonny Red's apartment.

ANDRES: "How did that work? What physically happened?"

LINO: "Usually you're at a table, and everybody holds hands and we say something in Italian, and you can't talk about anything that is discussed then until we break hands."

ANDRES: "Does anything else happen?"

LINO: "Well, at one time, they used to have a gun and a knife, but we did away with that." (Traditionally, the weapons would be placed on the table for dramatic effect.)

ANDRES: "Why is that no longer used?"

LINO: "Because the government was coming down on us too much."

ANDRES: "When you say 'the government' what do you mean?"

LINO: "The FBI."

JUDGE GARAUFIS: "I'm sorry. They were coming down on you with respect to what when you were having the ceremony?"

LINO: "They knew things were happening and we had to be careful."

ANDRES: "You mentioned at the ceremony, there are certain rules. What rules exist in organized crime?"

LINO: "Well, once you're a made member, you are not allowed to disrespect a member's wife or daughter, you can't cooperate with the government, and if you are called to a meeting, you can't carry a gun."

ANDRES: "If you are called to a meeting and you choose not to go?"

LINO: "You'll be gone."

ANDRES: "When you say 'You'll be gone'?"

LINO: "You're dead."

ANDRES: "In addition to your induction, did anyone else get inducted into the Bonanno Family that night?"

LINO: "Yes. Joey D'Amico, Big Trinny, maybe another seven, eight guys."

ANDRES: "Can you describe the ceremony that night?"

LINO: "We were called one by one into a room. We sat down and locked hands; they explained to us whatever we said now remains here—don't discuss it, you know. They would tell us what our obligation was as a made man. They gave you a chance—if you didn't want to get made, you could leave. I accepted it."

Colombo soldier Carmine "Tutti" Francese rushed into J&S Cake. He and Joey Massino were old pals. But Francese wasn't there to reminisce about happy times. He had alarming news: Sonny Red and his crew, he said, were "loading up." Word on the street was that the Red Team was buying up automatic weapons and was "getting ready for war." Francese had heard Red talking about finishing what Galante started, taking back the Family from Rastelli.

Massino knew he had only one option: a preemptive strike. But just killing Sonny Red wouldn't be enough—he'd have to brush aside all his enemies in one hit.

Armed with the talk of war, Massino approached bosses from two of the Five Families: Paul Castellano, head of the Gambinos, and Carmine "Junior" Persico, head of the Colombo Family. "They said, 'You have to defend yourself, do what you have to do,'" Massino later confided. (The Genoveses, the biggest and most powerful family in New York, were another story. Massino would later learn they backed the Red Team.) Having gotten Castellano's okay, Massino and Sal Vitale—the only one of his soldiers who knew of the plan to murder the three captains—made an appointment with the infamous Gambino underboss Aniello Dellacroce, who had worked for the legendary big boss Carlo Gambino, the family's namesake. The connection would prove to be vital to Massino's plan, as the Gambinos, in particular John Gotti, would play a significant role in the murders. (Gotti's crew was recruited to dispose of the bodies.) Massino's master stroke, however, was recruiting the Zips, the Bonnano's bloodthirsty Sicilian faction. They were a force unto themselves—young, hardened killers with no particular loyalties to anyone. Massino met with Zip captain Santo Giordano, and the two men came to an agreement: the Zips would be triggermen. Giordano would recruit two Montreal Zips to be the shooters. After the murders, they would immediately cross the border, so it would be nearly impossible to trace them.

There were only two more pieces of the puzzle to go: where and when. For the execution chamber, Massino chose a building in Dyker Heights, Brooklyn, once an after-hours club operated by Gambino henchman Sammy "The Bull" Gravano. The two-story, red-brick building looked like a small warehouse. It had a discreet entrance and was protected by an eight-foot-high steel fence. Massino decided he would kill the captains on a Tuesday, the day the Brooklyn and Queens Bonannos usually ate dinner at J&S Cake. It would be the perfect alibi—Massino and his men could slip away and return without raising suspicion. Last but not least, Sonny Black was given the job of luring the Red Team into Brooklyn: he simply called another meeting of the Bonanno captains. As far as

Sonny Red knew, the Commission's orders still held. No gunplay.

Early on the morning of May 5, 1981, Sal Vitale met Goldie at J&S Cake and told the kid to follow him to a location in Brooklyn. Goldie had no clue why, but did as he was told. The two made the thirty-minute drive from Maspeth to Dyker Heights. When they reached Thirteenth Avenue between Sixty-seventh and Sixty-eighth streets, they stopped. "I need that spot over there," said Sal through the window to Goldie, pointing to a parked car down the block. A few minutes later, a man returned to the car and drove away, allowing Vitale to pull his orange station wagon into position directly outside Sammy Bull's old club. Then Vitale jumped into Goldie's car, and the two returned to J&S Cake.

It was a busy day at the club. There were the usual suspects: Goldie, Tutti Francese and Big Louie. Sonny Black was there with some of his men. But there were unfamiliar faces too, Zips in particular. Sal Vitale was in and out, going for walk-talks and then returning. The men could sense something big was going down, but they knew better than to ask what. Late in the afternoon, Massino arrived with two Zips, Gerlando Sciascia and Santo Giordano. When he introduced them to Goldie, both the Sicilians screwed up their faces in disapproval. "He's a good kid," Massino reassured them. "Don't worry about it." Massino turned to Goldie and told him he was going to work the radios. He gave a nod to Vitale, who handed him a walkie-talkie and a police frequency scanner. "All right," Massino finally said, "let's go. We're going to straighten this thing out."

Around 6 p.m. on the same evening, the Red Team assembled at Sonny Red's place on Elizabeth Street, Little Italy. The mood was uneasy: another meeting had been called, and the captains knew there might be trouble—Sonny Red told his son Bruno Indelicato to "kill everybody" if he didn't come back. The three captains and Frank Lino set off for the first designated meeting point, the Sage Diner in Elmhurst, Queens. Lino took Big Trin in his car; Phil Lucky drove Sonny Red. When they arrived at the diner, they met two Zips aligned with Massino's faction, who were there to escort the captains to the meeting place in Brooklyn. The convoy drove to the parking lot of Nathan's Famous restaurant in south Brooklyn; the Red Team was told to leave their cars there and ride with the Zips the rest of the way to Sammy Bull's old club, only a mile away. As they walked inside, Frank Lino heard Sonny Red's instructions in the back of his mind: "If there's shooting, everybody is on his own. Try to get out."

Four vehicles set off from J&S Cake around 6 p.m. Massino and Vitale went in one car, Giordano and Sciascia drove another, and Goldie took his own; Sonny Black and Big Louie drove a van supplied by Goldie. Massino was headed north on Rust Street when Vitale noticed a suspicious car glide past, slow down and make a U-turn. "I think we've got a tail on," Vitale told Massino. "It's too late," the boss replied. "Try to lose him in traffic." They slowed down as Goldie pulled up beside them. "Watch yourself," Massino told him. "We just spotted a bad car." Massino's counter-surveillance skills were impeccable—there was in fact an FBI agent in the car. Agent Ted Savadel had been on his way home when he decided to make a pass by J&S Cake. As he cruised by, he saw Massino with a group of men he didn't recognize. Savadel gave chase as Massino and his crew drove away, but the mobsters were too quick. Vitale sped to the Brooklyn-Queens Expressway and turned west toward Brooklyn. By the time he reached the Kosciuszko Bridge, his rearview mirror was clear.

The convoy kept in touch via walkie-talkies during the tense, thirty-minute drive. Sonny Black complained over the air that Goldie's van was difficult to steer (the power-steering line had a habit of popping off.) A little muscle was all that was required, Goldie replied on the radio. They arrived in Dyker Heights at dusk. Vitale pulled up to the club, dropped Massino off at the curb and parked a couple of blocks up the street, near Sonny Black's van. Goldie parked just out of sight of the club, two blocks to the north, near the corner of busy Sixty-fifth Street. His instructions were to keep a lookout, stay low and listen to the scanner. If the police showed up, he was to alert the others immediately. He was still clueless about what he was doing there.

Just inside the door of the club was a small foyer, a coatroom and a larger storage room, about twenty by twenty feet. A flight of stairs led from the foyer to the clubroom above. Massino handed out the guns: the

Zips got a pistol apiece, and Vitale got a tommy gun. The clip was in position, and he assumed it was loaded. He fumbled with the safety catch, slapped the hammer into a place, pulled the trigger—and got the shock of his life. The small room was shaken with the rat-tat-tat of automatic gunfire. He just missed a Zip, and left five neat holes in the opposite wall. "If you don't have to fire, don't," Massino huffed. "I don't need bullets flying all over the room."

The four shooters hid in the coatroom in ski masks. Once the three captains passed by and entered the storeroom, Sciascia, who was to be positioned at the front door, would give a signal by running his hand through his hair. The shooters would then burst out of hiding and put the Red Team up against the wall, acting like it was a holdup; Vitale would guard the door behind them. If Sonny Red wasn't with them, Massino instructed, the hit was off. Red was key. And if Frank Lino got in the way, the shooters were to kill him too.

It was time. The men crouched inside the coatroom, saying nothing. The silence was broken only by the sound of shallow breaths. Each passing minute felt like an hour.

* * *

Goldie waited in his car, listening to the static on the scanner. It had grown dark—the local town houses were quiet, and the shops were deserted. He hadn't moved from his corner for three hours. He glanced at the spot where the orange station wagon sat in his rearview mirror; it seemed like he'd flicked his eyes up and back a thousand times. Boredom and fatigue were starting to set in. Finally, a voice came over the walkie-talkie. "Are you out of sight?" Goldie replied in the affirmative. "All right. Keep your eyes open. Have you heard anything?" No, he hadn't. "Are you sure? Nothing came over the scanner?" No, nothing. A moment later, the walkie-talkie came to life again. He recognized Sonny Black's voice. "The guys are here."

Gerlando Sciascia ushered the Red Team into the club. They strode the length of the foyer, about ten feet, and walked into the storeroom, where Massino and his crew were waiting. The team walked in and started to mingle. Big Trin and Lino chatted to Sciascia; Phil Lucky and Massino spoke on the other side of the room. Lucky held onto Massino's arm—a sign of Italian civility. For a moment, it seemed they were one happy family. But then, Sciascia gave the signal. There was a rush of footsteps, and a blur of black faces slammed into the room. Hell had crashed their party.

"Don't anybody move!" screamed one of the Zips. "This is a holdup." Big Trin's eyes widened. He charged, screaming, but his huge frame collided with a bullet. He fell in a heap. Frank Lino bolted, leapt over Big Trin's body and flew past Vitale, who was late in taking his position at the door. Massino belted Phil Lucky; Sonny Red started to run, but he only got a few feet before he was shot once and then again. He fell through the door. Sciascia pulled a pistol from his belt, pressed the barrel to Sonny Red's head and pulled the trigger. In the hail of crossfire, Santo Giordano was accidentally hit in the back and crumbled. Massino was firing too, pumping rounds into Big Trin. Phil Lucky was trapped against a wall. The gunmen turned and unloaded like a firing squad.

Frankie Lino sat forward in his seat, leaning over his microphone. His face was flushed—the storm of gunfire didn't feel like twenty-three years ago. So often, he'd run the miracle of his escape through his mind. But

if you'd told him that one day he'd be repeating his or-
deal in the witness box, he'd never have believed you.
The crowd in the courtroom could hardly believe it, either. They fell silent as Lino described what happened
next. Massino removed a piece of stale gum from his
mouth and wrapped it in a piece of scrap paper.

LINO: "When I got out, I . . . I ran, and I, you know, I
    jumped over some people's fences and I went into
    some people's homes."

ANDRES: "Okay. What's the last thing you saw before
    you left the club that day?"

LINO: "Well, I saw—the last thing I saw, I saw Phil
    Lucky get killed. Trinny and Sonny Red."

ANDRES: "You said you ran out the door. Where did
    you go?"

LINO: "I ran up the block on Sixty-eighth Street, jumped
    some fences and I knocked at a door and some peo-
    ple let me in their house."

ANDRES: "What did you do next?"

LINO: "I told them if I could use their phone, that I
    wouldn't hurt them, you know, and would they let
    me use their phone?"

ANDRES: "Whom did you call?"

LINO: "I called up some friends in My Way Lounge, and then I called up my house and I got my son Frankie on the phone."

ANDRES: "Did someone come and get you?"

LINO: "Yeah. My son Frankie showed up first."

ANDRES: "Where did you go?"

LINO: "From there, I called up Frank Coppa and I told him to meet me in Staten Island at my sister's, and he met me there."

ANDRES: "After you left the social club on that day, did you ever see Sonny Red Indelicato again?"

LINO: "No."

ANDRES: "After you left the social club on that day, did you ever see Phil Lucky Giaccone again?"

LINO: "No."

ANDRES: "After you left the social club on that day, did you ever see Dominic Trinchera again?"

(Pause.)

JUDGE: "You have to answer the question."

LINO: "No." (He said through tears.)

Not five minutes after Goldie heard Sonny Black's voice crackle over the radio, he saw men streaming out of the club. A Cadillac screeched to a stop by the door; Goldie watched two men drag another man into the back. (It was the wounded Giordano. He was left a paraplegic.) The car took off down the street. Goldie's walkie-talkie came alive again. "Did you get the guy that got out?" a voice asked, referring to Lino. "What guy?" screamed another voice. "Where were you?" inquired the first voice. "We're in the van," said the second. "What are you doing in the van?" snapped the first voice. "You were supposed to be standing outside the door once they came in." More waiting, and then a question directed to Goldie: "Did you hear anything come over the scanner?" Goldie radioed back, "No."

Inside the club, Vitale was barking orders. Sonny Red's body lay in the foyer; Phil Lucky and Big Trin were sprawled in the storeroom. Massino's team rolled the corpses up in drop cloths and tied them up with cord, and then dragged them to the front door. Vitale told Big Louie to pick up the bullet shells. There was blood everywhere. While the men cleaned up, Massino and Sonny Black talked outside about their biggest problem: Frankie Lino. He could go to the cops or, worse, alert the rest of Sonny Red's crew. They couldn't even worry about disposing of the bodies until they got to Lino. If he opened his mouth to anyone, they were finished.

Goldie heard Vitale's voice come over the radio. "We're going to move the van and take the car. You've got to follow behind." Goldie could see him in the mirror, pulling the station wagon out from its spot; the van took the wagon's place right outside the door to the club. Vitale and a couple other guys piled into Goldie's car, and Sal gave the order to drive up to Sixty-fifth Street, to where more men were waiting. Two of Sonny Black's men, including Benjamin "Lefty Guns" Ruggiero, were sitting in a parked car. They got out and jumped in the back of Goldie's car, and they all drove back to the club. The reinforcements went inside the club as Goldie and Vitale stood guard on either end of the block. They had the street completely cordoned off.

A voice on the walkie-talkie said, "We're coming out." Three carpetlike bundles were carried to the van. Big Louie jumped into the driver's seat and sped away; Goldie and Vitale followed him back to Queens. It was 3 a.m. by the time they reached Ozone Park. John Gotti's crew, including Gotti's brother Gene, were waiting in a desolate spot. Big Louie gave them the keys and got in with Vitale and Goldie. "Where to now?" asked Goldie. "In the opposite direction of that van," Sal replied.

It was another hour before Goldie returned to his apartment in Middle Village, Queens. He was getting ready for bed when the phone rang. It was Massino. "Are you by yourself? You don't have your girlfriend living with you anymore?" "No," said Goldie. "Right, I'm coming over." A few minutes later, the doorbell rang. Massino was at the door, along with three Canadian Zips, including Gerlando Sciascia. "Come on in, guys," said Massino, making himself at home. "Look how nice it is." The Zips sat on the floor in the living room, speaking to each other in Italian. Goldie went to his room and switched on the TV. The last thing he remembers before he drifted off was Massino sitting on the end of his bed, flipping the channels.

When Frank Lino landed on his sister's Staten Island doorstep that night, he had one thing on his mind: getting the hell to Pennsylvania. He called his old friend Frank Coppa, a Bonanno, and asked him to come over. When he arrived, Coppa found Lino in a state of shock. "They killed them," he was babbling. "They wore hoods, and I ran and ran." Coppa calmed him down, and managed to convince him to come back to his place. Not twenty minutes after they arrived, the telephone rang. "Pick up the phone," yelled Coppa. "It's your cousin, Eddie." Massino had contacted Eddie, a Gambino, in an attempt to reach Lino. "Come in," Eddie told him. "Don't worry, we just want to talk to you." Lino agreed, and returned to his sister's, where the crew was waiting for him: Gambino underboss Aniello Dellacroce, and Eddie. John Gotti's grave diggers were also there.

Dellacroce tried to reassure the terrified Lino. He explained the only reason he hadn't been told about the hit was because Sonny Red might have found out. "Now, Frank," he said, "did you go to the cops?" No, he hadn't. Nodding, Dellacroce turned to one of the men and told him to go "clean up." There were still three bodies to be buried that night. But Dellacroce wasn't finished. "Have you spoken to Bruno [Sonny Red's son]?" No, Lino replied. "Do you know where to find Bruno?" This time, Lino lied when he replied no. "That's a shame," replied Dellacroce. They were willing to offer Lino an ironclad insurance policy on his own life. They had a job for the lone survivor of the Red Team and the only person Bruno trusted: they wanted Lino to find the kid, and kill him.

Assistant U.S. Attorney Greg Andres sprang to his feet. Massino's defense attorney David Breitbart had just finished his grueling cross-examination of Frank Lino. Most people in the courtroom, including Judge Garaufis, were exhausted, but the young prosecutor still had plenty of enthusiasm. Andres strode from the prosecution table to the lectern and launched into his redirect.

ANDRES: "Mr. Lino, do you remember, during cross-examination, that Mr. Breitbart asked you certain questions about what happens when you get an order from a superior in an organized crime family?"

LINO: "Yes."

ANDRES: "So, for example, if a boss gives an order, does the soldier have to follow that order?"

LINO: "Yes."

ANDRES: "What are the penalties for a soldier if the soldier doesn't follow the order?"

LINO: "You know, you can get killed."

ANDRES: "If Joseph Massino, the boss of the Bonanno Crime Family, ordered people to attend this trial to intimidate you, would they have to attend?"

BREITBART: "Objection!"

JUDGE GARAUFIS: "That's sustained."

ANDRES: "If they attend on their own?"

BREITBART: "Move to strike."

JUDGE GARAUFIS: "The question is stricken. The jury will disregard it. Next."

ANDRES: "You testified that your son Joseph was a member of the Bonanno Crime Family, is that correct?"

LINO: "Yes."

ANDRES: "During the course of your testimony last Tuesday, did you see him in the courtroom?"

LINO: "Yes."

BREITBART: "Objection, Your Honor. This is not correct. I didn't ask him any questions about his son Joseph."

JUDGE GARAUFIS: "Sustained. The jury will disregard it. Let's move to something else."

ANDRES: "During the time you were in jail in 1999, do you know if a made member of the Bonanno Family had ever agreed to testify in court?"

BREITBART: "Objection!"
JUDGE GARAUFIS: "Sidebar."

The day after the murder, every surviving member of the Bonanno Family made their way to Massino's new home in Howard Beach. The chief welcomed them like a newly crowned monarch, standing on the threshold of untold power and wealth. Massino was now the strongest captain in the Family, and the closest link to its incarcerated boss, Rusty Rastelli. Soon, word began to reach the other families. But Massino made a point of telling the Genoveses personally. He and Sciascia paid Vincent "The Chin" Gigante a visit. When they arrived at his downtown Manhattan social club, Sciascia waited outside while Massino went in to speak to his rival. Gigante's minder asked Massino to sit. "I'm not sitting," Massino replied. A man at his level didn't have to lower himself before anyone.

Rusty Rastelli still had the title. But after that night, the New York underworld had a new boss: Joseph Massino.

FOUR

ON THE LAM

Six days after her husband disappeared, Annette Giaccone and her attorney, George Faber, walked into the 2nd Police Precinct in Suffolk County, Long Island, New York, to file a missing persons report. In the space for "nickname," she wrote "Lucky," but it seemed Philip Giaccone's luck had run out. She reported to the officer on duty that her husband had left for work on the previous Tuesday at approximately 10 a.m. "He did not appear nervous," the officer wrote, per her statements. "He made no complaints to her, nor did she suspect anything was wrong." She noted he was driving a 1979 blue Lincoln town car. A heavyset white male accompanying Mrs. Giaccone added that the license plate number was 247. He said he remembered it "because I often play that number." The officer filed his report, and then relayed the information to his federal counterparts. But the FBI was already hard at work on Phil Lucky's case—in fact, they knew he and the others were dead within hours of the shootings. A brave undercover agent planted deep inside the Bonanno Family had phoned in the news. His name was Joseph Pistone, but in the underworld, he was known as Donnie Brasco.

I met Joseph Pistone aka Donnie Brasco in a bodega on the gritty West Side of Midtown Manhattan. Considering what he'd done he looked unremarkable: not quite six feet tall, with a stocky build. His receding hairline had left him with a kind, round face. But it was his eyes—quiet and intense—that gave him away. Before me stood an FBI legend, the man who had spent six years inside a New York Mafia family. No sooner had we sat down with coffee and bagels than two burly Italians sat down at the table beside us; Pistone immediately got up and moved us to a table out of earshot. He said it was because they were too noisy, but I suspected he just didn't want them to overhear us. Speaking in a thick New York accent, he talked about life in the mob in the same matter-of-fact tone he used to order his bagel, and was prone to cutting short his stories by saying, "you know, the whole megillah." But it didn't matter. Joseph Pistone was a man whose reputation preceded him.

Pistone is considered to be the most successful undercover agent the FBI has ever produced. In 1975, he started hanging out in bars frequented by criminals, posing as a jewel thief. Using only a hidden tape recorder and his wits, he slowly worked his way into the Bonanno Family. He breathed their air, ate dinner in their homes and pretended to conspire with their crimes. If at any moment he had been discovered, or even suspected, he would have been killed. Nevertheless, when I asked him if he was scared, he calmly replied, "No. If I had been, I would have made a mistake. It's a case of knowing what these guys are capable of. You should always know your opponent. I knew these guys are like anybody else, except they'd kill you."

Growing up Italian in blue-collar Paterson, New Jersey, Pistone saw many of the neighborhood kids turn out to be gangsters, so pretending to be one was like living out what might have been. He was so good at his job that he was actually nominated for membership by his Mafia pals—he almost became a made man. Pistone resurfaced from his undercover work in 1981, before he reached that point, but by then he'd collected enough tape to deliver a crippling blow to the Bonannos. His testimony helped put roughly two hundred mobsters in prison.

The story of how the FBI told the Bonannos about Brasco's real identity has become legend in the Mafia world: on July 28, 1981, the Feds turned up at Bonanno captain Sonny Black's apartment in Greenpoint, Brooklyn, and showed him a photograph of Brasco standing alongside four other agents. Black is said to have simply replied, "So?" But a famous series of surveillance photographs shows Sonny Black and his crew members standing outside the club in shocked disbelief a few minutes later.

The world first heard Donnie Brasco's story in August 1982, when Pistone appeared on the witness stand to testify against five members of Sonny Black's crew. More than 150 spectators crammed into Room 318 of the Manhattan Federal Courthouse to hear Pistone spill his stories. "Let's face it," he said to me. "It was the first major trial where mob guys had been indicted for murder under RICO (Racketeer Influenced and Corrupt

Organizations Act, 1970), and it was the first trial where an undercover had spent so long in the mob." Overnight he went from being a secret agent—whose work was little known even to his wife—to being a hero and media star. It seemed the press was even more aggressive than the mob in pursuing him. "My name was splashed all over," he recalled. "Reporters and TV people were calling FBI headquarters looking to get in touch with me. I had to move my family, the whole megillah." Pistone resisted going public until he published his 1989 book entitled *Donnie Brasco: My Life Inside the Mafia,* which became the basis for the film *Donnie Brasco* starring Johnny Depp and Al Pacino. In preparation for his role, Depp spent months tagging along behind Pistone, copying his street-speak and tough-guy mannerisms. "I tell you what," Pistone said of Depp, "there's one good kid."

The Bonanno Family was deeply embarrassed by the Brasco incident, and tried to stop Pistone from testifying by putting a five-hundred-thousand-dollar price on his head. Pistone, his wife and his three daughters have lived in hiding ever since, moving frequently and never discussing their past with friends or family. The former undercover agent tries to avoid New York, but he admitted he occasionally wanders into Little Italy to sample the cuisine. "If I bump into an old-timer, I'm not too worried," he said, "but these young guys today are so volatile and violent. You might get some guy who thinks he's going to be some fucking hero cowboy, you know. I watch out for that." When I asked if he still carried a gun, he looked at me dead in the eyes.

"I carry."

News that an agent had penetrated the Family reached Goldie months before it hit the headlines. It was the summer of 1981; as he was walking toward J&S Cake, Sal Vitale stopped him in the street. "You're never going to believe this one," said Vitale. "Sonny Black's crew had an agent with them." "What?!" replied Goldie. "Yeah," said Sal, "come on inside." The men walked into the dimly lit club, where a group of brooding gangsters was standing at the bar, among them Joey Massino and Tutti Francese. Massino showed Goldie a photograph of the agent. "Do you know this guy?" he asked, pointing at the photo. "No," said Goldie, "I never saw him before in my life." "He's been around Sonny for six years," replied Massino.

It was a mighty blow. Sonny Black was Massino's number-one ally and business partner, not to mention his collaborator in the murder of the three captains. But still, believing that an agent had been walking among them was almost impossible. How could it have happened? What did it mean? The repercussions were endless—anyone who'd done business with Sonny Black was vulnerable. But there was nothing they could do. They could practically hear the indictments being typed up in the Manhattan U.S. Attorney's Office all the way from Maspeth.

At that moment, Massino and his men were in a far worse predicament than they realized. The FBI had planted at least four bugs on phone lines in Bonanno Family haunts across the city; their undercover man was still in so deep that Sonny Black gave *him* the contract to hit the last surviving member of the Red Team, Sonny Red's son Bruno, the same man Lino was first asked to kill. (It was not long after he got the murder contract that the FBI yanked Pistone off the street.) As word of Brasco's real identity reverberated through the underworld, the FBI listened carefully to their bugs as the gangsters blabbed about what to do. Once they intercepted a call to Benjamin "Lefty Guns" Ruggiero, who had been a close associate of Brasco's, telling him to go to a social club on Madison Avenue in Manhattan's Lower East Side. Thinking it might be a hit, the Feds arrested Ruggiero as he left his apartment building. That fall, they arrested four other Bonannos from Sonny Black's crew, indicting them on charges of conspiracy to murder the three captains, robbery, illegal gambling and drug dealing.

The arrests hit the Bonanno Family hard, and for Massino, frighteningly close to home. His family, the organization he had worked so hard to build, had been compromised by one of his most trusted associates. It was not a mistake he considered forgivable. Eventually, both Massino and Sonny Black were indicted as well, but by that time, they were both missing. Little did the FBI know, one of them was already sleeping with the fishes.

At Massino's 2004 trial, Frank Lino testified under cross-examination about his encounter with the FBI mole. It came to light that Massino had suspected Brasco for some time. But to the rest of the Bonannos, Brasco had been just what he wanted to be: virtually unknown.

Gerlando "George from Canada" Sciascia, the Bonanno captain who ran the Family's Montreal crew. He was murdered in 1999 on Massino's orders.

Sciascia was found dead in a Bronx alley after going to a meeting at a diner. A bullet hole was where his left eye should have been.

Photos courtesy of the U.S. Attorney's Office unless noted otherwise.

Massino at the Little Italy haunt Toyland in the '70s. The social club was operated by then-consigliere Steve "Stevie Beef" Cannone.

Joseph Massino as a young man. He started his mob career as a truck hijacker, a close associate to Queens counterpart John Gotti in the '70s.

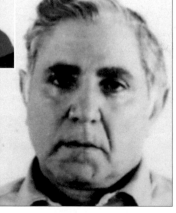

Phillip "Rusty" Rastelli was the Bonanno Family boss from the late '60s until he died in 1991. He groomed Massino to be his successor.

Salvatore "Good-Looking Sal" Vitale was Massino's brother-in-law, underboss, and ultimately, his betrayer.

Anthony Spero

Sal Vitale and Anthony Spero, Massino's consigliere, ran the Family in the early '90s when Massino was serving a five-year prison term for labor racketeering.

Massino and Colombo gangster Carmine "Tutti" Francese in the '70s.

Massino's '70s house on Caldwell Avenue in Maspeth, Queens.
Photo by Simon Crittle

Photos courtesy of the U.S. Attorney's Office unless noted otherwise.

In the '70s, Massino used warehouses in the industrial area beside Newton Creek on the Brooklyn-Queens border to stash stolen trucks.
Photo by Simon Crittle

J&S Cake today. The Maspeth, Queens, social club was Massino's headquarters in the early '80s, and was once bugged by the FBI.
Photo by Simon Crittle

A lunch wagon in Maspeth, Queens. Massino ran a fleet of the vehicles, out of which his drivers would take illegal numbers bets at factories and truck stops.
Photo by Simon Crittle

Massino and his wife, Josephine. She held on to their faux-Georgian mansion in Howard Beach, Queens, after Massino was convicted of seven murders.

Massino's home in Howard Beach, Queens.
Photo by Simon Crittle

Photos courtesy of the U.S. Attorney's Office unless noted otherwise.

Duane "Goldie" Leisenheimer was a professional car thief and a key member of Massino's crew in the '70s and '80s. He testified against Massino in 2004.

Bonanno captain Dominick "Sonny Black" Napolitano. Black would later be killed for unwittingly allowing FBI agent Joseph Pistone, aka Donnie Brasco, to infiltrate the Family.

Alphonse "Sonny Red" Indelicato and his son Anthony "Bruno" Indelicato in Long Island in 1981, a few weeks before Sonny Red was gunned down on Massino's orders.

Sonny Red was found dead in a vacant lot in Ozone Park, Queens. More than twenty years later, the bodies of the two other captains from his faction were found in the same lot.

Phil "Lucky" Giaccone was once Massino's captain, but eventually died in the spray of bullets alongside Sonny Red.

Dominick "Big Trin" Trinchera, who was also killed with Sonny Red, charged the gunmen before being cut down. Massino was convicted of the triple murder in 2004.

The three captains were lured to this Brooklyn building, a former social club once operated by Sammy "The Bull" Gravano, and were then killed on the ground floor.
Photo by Simon Crittle

James "Big Louie" Tartaglione was one of Massino's most trusted captains in the '80s and '90s, but later turned informant for the FBI.

James Tartaglione

Goldie's parents' home in the Poconos, where Massino went into hiding.
Photo by Simon Crittle

Photos courtesy of the U.S. Attorney's Office unless noted otherwise.

A young Frank Lino (left) and Ronald "Monkey Man" Filocomo at dinner.

Frank Lino, a Brooklyn Bonanno, was involved in rackets from pornography to stock-market fraud. After turning cooperator, he admitted to multiple murders.

Frank Lino and Gabe Infanti, both senior mob figures, in the '70s. Infanti was rubbed out by Massino after he botched two hits.

Undercover agent Joseph Pistone (left) as Donnie Brasco with Sonny Black in Florida in 1980.

Agent Joseph Pistone (second from left) in the FBI photograph that was shown to Sonny Black and the rest of the Bonannos after Pistone was pulled off the street.

Photos courtesy of the U.S. Attorney's Office unless noted otherwise.

Sonny Black, just moments after he found out about Brasco, with his famed racing pigeons on the roof of his social club.

Sicilian Bonnano Cesare Bonventre (second from right), Anthony Mirra (third from right), and associates in the '70s.

Tony Mirra was shot several times in his car by his Bonanno cousin. Along with Sonny Black, Massino blamed Mirra for the Donnie Brasco fiasco.

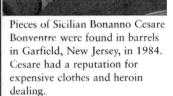

Pieces of Sicilian Bonanno Cesare Bonventre were found in barrels in Garfield, New Jersey, in 1984. Cesare had a reputation for expensive clothes and heroin dealing.

An X-ray of Cesare Bonventre's skull, showing the bullet still lodged in his head.

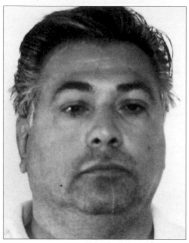

Richard Cantarella, a Bonanno captain, made millions in the parking-lot business. He flipped after being caught on tape recorder by his partner, Barry Weinberg.

Barry Weinberg started informing for the FBI in 2001. He would provide crucial pieces of evidence in the case that eventually brought Massino down.

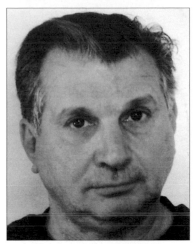

Sal Vitale's mug shot, after his arrest.

Massino on the day of his arrest in 2003. The last of the Five Family dons, he was convicted of seven murders in 2004 after his brother-in-law ratted him out.

Photos courtesy of the U.S. Attorney's Office unless noted otherwise.

An artist's rendering of the Last Godfather at his 2004 trial.
Drawing © Andrea Shepard

BREITBART: "Did you ever hear of the famous FBI agent by the name of Donnie Brasco?"

LINO: "Yes, I saw him in the movies."

BREITBART: "Did you ever meet him in the street?"

LINO: "Never."

BREITBART: "Did there come a time when you learned that Donnie Brasco investigated the Bonanno Family?"

LINO: "Well, I was told not to go to a wedding, because I was going to sit with him."

BREITBART: "Who told you that?"

LINO: "Joe Massino."

BREITBART: "Not to sit with Donnie Brasco?"

LINO: "No. We were going to a wedding—somebody in [Bonanno soldier John] Boobie Cerasani's family was getting married in Staten Island. A couple of days before the wedding, word was sent to me, don't go to the wedding because this Donnie Brasco might be bad."

BREITBART: "Did there come a time, sir, when you learned that the FBI went and visited many people to advise them that Donnie Brasco was an agent?"

LINO: "Yes. After he was taken off the street, they came to my pizzeria, the FBI, and they says, if you got any intentions of killing Donnie Brasco, forget it because he's an FBI agent and he infiltrated you guys. Tough luck, they told us."

BREITBART: "Did there come a time, sir, that you learned he was wearing a wire and tape-recording conversations?"

LINO: "Who was wearing a wire?"

BREITBART: "Brasco."

LINO: "I don't even know Donnie Brasco. If he walked in here now, I wouldn't even know unless it's Richard [sic Johnny] Depp."

Wanted: Field Information, read the headline of the NYPD poster. Underneath was a haphazard arrangement of dirt-covered men's clothing, including a dark pair of trousers, a dark V-neck T-shirt, a pair of slip-on leather shoes and a leather belt that was dried stiff and out of shape. To the right of the clothes was a close-up showing a metal bracelet with chunky, flat links. *The above is a photo of clothing and jewelry (worn on the right wrist), recovered from a decomposed body of an unidentified victim of a homicide, discovered 8-12-82 in a remote area within the confines of the 122 PCT,* said a caption. *The deceased was found wrapped in a*

Bellevue Hospital Mortuary Bag. Description: Adult Male. White. 5'6" to 5'7". Slim Build. Crime: Death by gunshot wound to head. Notify the Staten Island Crimes Against Persons Squad forthwith.

The grisly discovery was made by a man walking his dog in the woods of Staten Island. Photos taken by police at the scene showed a man's leg poking out of a creek bank. When the police pulled the soggy corpse out of the mud and laid it on a bed of leaves, it was unrecognizable. An autopsy conducted the next day found that the body was so decomposed and filthy, the skin color was difficult to determine. "The entire body is blackish in color, with tan-white greasy areas," said the medical examiner. "It is covered in brown mud and a few green and brown twigs and leaves." At first glance, the examiner even had trouble telling if the dead person was a man or a woman. "The external genitalia are consistent with those of a male. They are very friable and are falling apart on examination." The body's fingers were also missing.

The examiner proceeded to inspect the corpse's head. The eyeballs were sunken, the nose decomposed; the tongue was protruding from the mouth. A full body X-ray revealed "metallic fragments" inside the man's skull, which was then cut away for further inspection. A deformed bullet was found in the right frontal area of the brain. Eventually, the medical examiner was forced to resort to dental records to identify the body. Five days before Pistone would take the stand, the ME made his determination: the dead man was Dominick "Sonny Black" Napolitano.

Sonny Black had always felt most at ease when he was alone on the roof of his Motion Lounge club in Greenpoint, Brooklyn. It was there that he kept his prize possessions: pigeons. Besides being a bookie, a hijacker and a murderer, Sonny Black was a pigeon racer. He kept almost a hundred birds in his rooftop coops, some worth thousands of dollars each. The brilliantly colored creatures had pedigree bloodlines that descended from prize pigeons in France, Germany and Russia. In fact, Joseph Pistone remembers Sonny Black being more interested in his birds than his children, adding that pigeon racing was popular among New York wiseguys. "They take them to, say, North Carolina, put a clock on their legs and let them fly back to the coop," said Pistone. I remarked it was amazing the birds could find their way back home. In response, he deadpanned, "That's why they call them homing pigeons."

Sonny Black had dead-straight black hair, a square jaw and a Roman nose. Pistone recalled that he had a dry sense of humor and was always challenging Donnie Brasco to arm wrestling matches and losing. (He once spat in Brasco's face right as they began, just so he could beat him.) But Sonny Black was no gutter gangster: besides the odd glass of French liquor, he was neither a hard drinker nor a degenerate gambler. And unlike Pistone's close mob associate, Lefty Guns Ruggiero, who never stopped talking about the elusive big score, Sonny Black left his business behind once the workday was done. "Sonny was a stone-cold killer," he recalled, "but you could also sit and talk to him just normally."

Black wasn't freewheeling or flashy. To this day, the only reason he's remembered is because he was the hapless captain who allowed an agent to burrow into his family—a mistake for which he paid with his life. The question of who killed Sonny Black remained unanswered for more than twenty years after his death. Not until 2004 was it revealed that the man who ordered his murder was Joseph Massino.

* * *

Before the Donnie Brasco story exploded, Massino found another use for Frank Lino. Once word hit the street that Sonny Red was "gone," his crew had scattered in all directions, which meant there were half a dozen dangerous men on the loose whose last order was to retaliate if Sonny Red was touched. But Massino was done killing—it was bad for business. He proclaimed that if Red's men didn't come in shooting, old rivalries would be forgotten. Frank Lino was the man Massino recruited to spread the word. If he could bring them all in, Massino told him, he would remain a captain and his safety would be guaranteed. Lino cautiously agreed and went about tracking down the remainder of Sonny Red's crew. But his suspicion that Massino wanted him dead never left him—he still felt like he had something to prove. So when Massino offered him a murder contract, he jumped at the chance to show his loyalty.

Massino and Gerlando Sciascia arrived at Lino's Bensonhurst bar in mid-1981 to discuss the hit. Lino suggested they carry it out in a house owned by Ernest "Kippy" Filocomo, a Bonanno associate. Within days, Lino called a meeting with his crew on Avenue U in his

Brooklyn neighborhood. According to testimony, in attendance was his cousin Robert "Bobby" Lino, Frank Coppa and Kippy Filocomo. Lino tapped Bobby and Kippy's son Ronnie "Monkey Man" Filocomo, an associate of Coppa's, to be the shooters. (Ronnie would later plead guilty to Black's murder in exchange for a reduced jail sentence.) The only information he was able to give them about the hit was the little he'd been given by Massino: the target was the Bonanno who'd given Donnie Brasco access to the Family.

Sonny Black sat in the backseat of a car speeding across the Verrazano Bridge. He was leaving Brooklyn, his wife, his children and his beloved pigeons. It was dusk, and to the west clouds licked at the lights of the Manhattan Financial District's skyscrapers. A summer storm was gathering.

Frank Lino was driving the car; beside him, in the passenger seat, was Steve "Stevie Beef" Cannone, the chunky Family consigliere. Sonny Black sat in the back seat as Cannone did the talking. Permitting Sonny Black to live was unthinkable. He had allowed an FBI agent to infiltrate the Family, and now major indictments were expected to fall. He had embarrassed the Bonannos in front of the other New York families and reduced their century-old tradition to a joke. Every new breath he took prolonged their shame. When the car finally reached the Staten Island Expressway on the far side of the narrows, Sonny Black knew he'd never see Brooklyn again.

Mob lore has it that, earlier that day, Sonny had stopped in at the Motion Lounge. He gave his watch and other personal items to the bartender and said he'd been summoned to a meeting and didn't think he was coming back. Old-world Mafia code says if you are "called in" you have to go, and Sonny Black was a true believer. In his mind, the good of the Family was what mattered most. So he drove his 1979 black Coupe De Ville to a steak house in Bayridge, Brooklyn, and, as planned, met up with Stevie Beef. As consigliere—the third-highest rank in the Family—Cannone was supposedly someone Sonny Black could trust.

Meanwhile, at Kippy's house, Bonanno soldier Frank Coppa and half a dozen other Family men had just eaten a meal of fried chicken. The hit men started rearranging the furniture, setting up chairs and a table in the basement to make it look as if there was going to be a meet and greet. Bobby Lino was issued with a semiautomatic fitted with a silencer; Monkey Man got a revolver. The others loitered upstairs in the kitchen, milling around to make it seem like they were waiting for the crowded meeting to start. Frank Coppa waited by the door.

Lino quietly drove across Staten Island. As he pulled up to a traffic light, he glanced to his right; there at the curb, as planned, was a white delivery van. It was the backup car in case anything went wrong. Massino, Vitale and Sciascia were inside. Lino made eye contact with the men but said nothing before continuing on. The van followed well behind.

They reached Kippy's and parked outside. Lino, Sonny Black and Stevie Beef got out and walked up the steps to the front door. Lino rang the doorbell and Coppa answered. Everyone was downstairs, he said. He directed the men inside and to the right, where a door opened to a flight of steps that led to the basement. Lino went first, Sonny Black second. Coppa stopped Stevie Beef at the top of the stairs.

Lino had been too good a witness for David Breitbart's liking. He'd described the murder of the three captains in great detail, and also claimed that he'd organized

Sonny Black's homicide on Massino's orders. Breitbart knew he had to discredit Lino if his client were going to be acquitted. Just as he had done with the other co-operators, he badgered Lino on the stand.

BREITBART: "Now, there came a time when you were going down the steps."

LINO: "As I was walking down maybe four steps, somebody slammed the door that was upstairs. When Sonny heard the door slam, he turned and that's when I grabbed him by the shoulder and threw him down the steps."

BREITBART: "You just made a motion with your arm; is that the arm you used?"

LINO: "I couldn't be sure if it was my left arm or my right."

BREITBART: "Are you some kind of a judo champion that you were able to throw him over your shoulder?"

ANDRES: "Objection."

JUDGE GARAUFIS: "Sustained. Ask him what happened."

BREITBART: "Were you in better shape then?"

LINO: "Yes, I was a weight lifter."

BREITBART: "You grabbed him by the shirt. Did he tumble down?"

LINO: "He just lost his balance and fell down to the basement."

BREITBART: "Was he on his back or belly?"

LINO: "He was, like, on his knees."

BREITBART: "Who shot first?"

LINO: "Bobby shot him first. Then when he went to shoot him a second time the gun jammed."

BREITBART: "How far away from the body of the individual were the guns placed?"

LINO: "Maybe two feet?"

BREITBART: "This was not a matter of target practice, this was an execution, right?"

LINO: "Yes."

BREITBART: "Now, after that happened, did you see Ronnie Filocomo do something?"

LINO: "Ronnie walked over. He had a different type of gun that made a lot of noise. He shot him once more and Sonny went down. Then he says, 'Hit me once more, make it good.' "

Upstairs Frank Coppa had heard a gunshot, a pause and then two more. Less than a minute had passed since he'd slammed the door. He opened it again and looked down to the basement. At the bottom of the stairs, he saw Sonny Black on the ground, his head lying in a pool of blood. Coppa yelled down to Lino to get Black's keys out of his pocket—they would need them to get rid of his car, parked back in Brooklyn. Lino went through the dead man's pockets and found the keys, as well as a wallet. It contained a couple of snapshots and one hundred dollars. Kippy took the money.

The crew went to work. They quickly zipped Sonny Black inside a black bag Lino had gotten from a funeral home in Bensonhurt. The body bag had BELLEVUE HOSPITAL printed on its side in white block letters. Then they loaded up the body and made a beeline for the gravesite in the woods. Coppa went in one car, a Cadillac, and the other men took the body in another. By then, storm clouds had closed in, and it was raining. Coppa lost the other car in traffic. Meanwhile, at the gravesite, his associates couldn't find the pre-dug hole in the darkness. As their frustration grew, so did their paranoia about being stopped by police. They found a muddy spot beside a creek in what looked like a wilderness, and buried Sonny Black.

* * *

The small, two-story house in the Pocono Mountains was obscured by pine trees. Set back roughly a hundred feet from the road, it was painted a reddish brown, with white window edges and shutters. A short flight of steps led up to a wooden deck surrounding the house, as well as a sliding glass entrance. At the top of the driveway hung a sign presenting the name *Leisenheimer* in cursive letters. The house, located roughly five miles outside the tourist town of Milford, Pennsylvania, about two hours' drive from New York City, belonged to Goldie's parents.

After Donnie Brasco surfaced in 1981, Massino got word that his name was going to be attached to a major federal indictment: he was facing a long prison stretch on charges including conspiracy to murder the three captains and truck hijacking. He knew he'd stand a better chance of beating the case if he were tried separately from the other Bonannos. But for that to happen, he'd have to avoid arrest until his charges were severed from the rest of the group. The Chief would have to go into hiding.

In early 1982, when Massino was still trying to

figure out where to go, he summoned Goldie to J&S Cake. "Listen," he told the kid, "I need a place to stay for about thirty days." Goldie said he was sure he could find a spot. "What about your parents' place?" Massino continued. Goldie hesitated. "Like you said," he replied. "It's my parents' place. I'll ask my father." Massino instructed him to tell his father they needed the house to "duck a subpoena." Goldie and Massino skipped town in March. A week after they fled, the first indictments fell, and Sonny Black's old crew was rounded up.

As Massino's fugitive weeks turned into months, Vitale made regular trips to Milford, as did a handful of other captains (and even John Gotti, who also had a house in the area). It was Goldie's job to escort them to the house—he'd sit at the scalloped counter of the Milford Diner, waiting for them to arrive. Then he'd lead the mobsters up the hill to his parents' house, making sure nobody was following. Once there, he'd stand guard outside while they talked to the boss. When visits weren't possible, Massino kept in contact with Vitale over the phone: they had devised a system to avoid being picked up on bugs. Before Massino left New York, he gave Vitale five phone numbers in Queens. They were given letters, A through E. Each time they spoke, Massino told him the letter of the next phone he was going to call, and the time he would call it.

Not every moment of Massino's time in Milford was spent on the job—he made sure he was getting plenty of recreation. He often drove across the New York border to the town of Port Jervis, where he shopped for chocolates and china dolls for his daughters and had them shipped back to the city by the store owner—slipping her an extra $100 to leave the return address off the packages, so the FBI couldn't track them. When Goldie's parents stayed at the house on weekends, Massino moved down to the Mount Haven Resort at the bottom of the hill. Three Italian brothers, originally from Queens, owned the hotel, and they made Massino feel right at home. Massino befriended one of the brothers, Anthony Filone. He told Filone his name was Joseph Russo and that he owned a bowling alley in New York. The two men shared a passion for food, and Filone often prepared Italian specialties for Massino. Anthony has since died, but his brother Andrew recalls of Massino, "His whole life was food. He and my brother used to create dishes together. Joe would bring in food and ask us to cook it. He'd even have food shipped up from New York." Massino told the brothers he left New York because of stress and his weight problem. "He was always kidding around with the waitresses," said Filone. "He was a character."

Linda Lucci led a typical life. She grew up in Queens; after graduating from high school, she learned clerical skills at Drake Business School in Astoria. At twenty she married a deadbeat, who promptly landed himself in prison. Meeting a guy like Joseph Massino was the most exciting thing that ever happened to her.

It was the summer of 1976. She was a beautiful twenty-four-year-old Italian girl, slim, with long dark hair, standing at just five-foot-three. To her, Massino (then thirty-three) was fascinating—she was impressed by the way people gravitated toward him, and she could tell he was important. Everyone wanted to know Massino, and now she did too. Ray Wean, who lived in Lucci's building, first introduced her to Massino at J&J Catering. At the time, Lucci's husband was incarcerated in Dannemora Prison in upstate New York, where Rastelli was also in prison. Massino regularly traveled upstate to see Rastelli, and said he was happy to give her a ride as well. Of course, she knew better than to ask Massino what his business there was.

The affair between Lucci and Massino seemed almost inevitable. Their weekends away became a regular occurrence; after Rastelli was transferred from Dannemora to Lewisburg in Pennsylvania, Lucci continued to accompany Massino on his trips to see him. They stayed in hotels, and he took her out to what seemed to her to be fancy restaurants. She was still having an affair with Massino when she divorced her husband in 1979. In 1980, she and Massino broke up. She never expected to see or hear from him again.

Two years later she got a call—it was Massino. After many months on the run from the law, he'd got to thinking about her. The Poconos, of course, had long been a cliché for romance, and there he was, with only Goldie to keep him occupied. His wife, Josephine, was at home with the children and the FBI had her under surveillance, so she was no good to him. Linda Lucci, however, was unknown to the Feds. She agreed to meet him at Cesare's Pocono Palace for a weekend tryst.

The landmark resort had a sign midway along its tree-lined entrance road that read, YOU ARE ENTERING

THE LAND OF LOVE. Massino and Lucci joined the couples wandering the grounds and doing laps on the roller-skating rink, staying in suites featuring red carpet, heart-shaped Jacuzzis and beds surrounded by mirrors. For extra-special occasions, the palace offered rooms with seven-foot-high bubble baths shaped like champagne glasses. Massino would settle for nothing but the best.

At the trial, Massino's affair with Linda Lucci was revealed. The prosecution used Lucci's testimony to corroborate the fact that Massino had been in the Poconos. Massino's wife, Josephine, a fixture in the gallery, stared at the floor as her husband's amorous weekends were detailed to the jury. Lucci, however, was spared the embarrassment—the government didn't subpoena her. Instead, FBI agent Kim McCaffrey sat in the witness box and read from a deposition Lucci gave the government in 1984. Assistant U.S. Attorney Greg Andres played the role of interviewer.

ANDRES: "Did you begin to see him on a regular basis?"
McCAFFREY (LUCCI): "For a while, no. I did see him a week after that [initial] conversation."
ANDRES: "Did he tell you where he was living?"

McCAFFREY (LUCCI): "Yes. He was living for a time in motels, different motels."

ANDRES: "Were you aware that he was indicted in March of 1982?"

McCAFFREY (LUCCI): "Yes, I was."

ANDRES: "Did you discuss with him the fact that he had been indicted?"

McCAFFREY (LUCCI): "Not on the phone we didn't. When I saw him we did."

ANDRES: "Is this in motels in Pennsylvania?"

McCAFFREY (LUCCI): "Yes."

ANDRES: "Do you recall what motels he was living in or cities they were in?"

McCAFFREY (LUCCI): "He was moving. Whenever I would meet him, he would have enough clothing for the weekend, a few days."

ANDRES: "What did he say he had been indicted for?"

McCAFFREY (LUCCI): "Hijackings and conspiracy to murder."

ANDRES: "Did he ever mention a man by the name of Sonny Black Napolitano?"

McCAFFREY (LUCCI): "Yes."

ANDRES: "Do you recall what he said?"

McCAFFREY (LUCCI): "Just that he was on the lam."

* * *

The two fifty-gallon steel oil drums were found in a warehouse in Garfield, New Jersey, on April 16, 1984, covered in scratches and dents. When local police officers pried open the lids they found a man inside—one man inside two drums. They found his head and torso in the first. The man's legs were in the second, his feet pointing upward still clad in socks. "The lower legs, including the thigh, leg and foot, both right and left, were found in one drum," wrote the Bergen County medical examiner, "and the significantly decomposed trunk with the head was found in the other drum." He added that all the body parts were covered in a "whitish-grey, elastic-like, gummy substance." He recovered five bullets from the victim's skull, noting that the man had been dead for two or three weeks. It took three weeks more to figure out who the man was: using dental records and the dead man's gold crucifix necklace, the police determined that his name was Cesare Bonventre.

Bonventre had been a powerful captain in the Bonanno's Sicilian faction. He was a slick individual, tall and blond, who drove a blue Cadillac and wore a gold watch. He combed his hair back over his head and wore his shirt unbuttoned to expose his chest and crucifix. Bonventre was dapper, but he was also dangerous—he was a reputed narcotics dealer who was listed on the sweeping Pizza Connection indictment a week before his body was discovered. He was known for his tinted glasses, fitted shirts and his sudden outbursts of extreme violence. He made headlines in 1979 as one of Carmine Galante's two bodyguards who escaped without a scratch when Galante was cut down. After the murder, Rastelli promoted Bonventre, then in his twenties, to captain, along with Massino and Sonny Black.

In 1984, Massino moved out of Goldie's parents' house in Milford and went ten miles west along Interstate 84, to a gated community called Hemlock Farms. The heavily wooded, 4,500-acre community surrounded by state land and gun clubs was off limits to the public, and only had three entrances. Residents had to be cleared by a gatekeeper; and visitors had to have their names checked against a list before being admitted. There was a private police force, a kids' camp, ten tennis courts, three lakes and absolutely no stores or restaurants. It was the perfect place for Massino to lay low during the remainder of his days as a fugitive.

It was during his time at Hemlock Falls that Massino planned the murder of the only surviving captain from the old guard who still presented any threat to him. He'd already rubbed out Sonny Red, Big Trin, Phil Lucky and Sonny Black—now Cesare Bonventre had to go. With him out of the way, Massino would truly be the last man standing and have a clear path to succeed Rastelli to become the Family's official boss. Massino summoned Vitale and another trusted Bonanno lieutenant, Louie "HaHa" Attanasio. Attanasio was Bonventre's acting captain, and after lunch, Massino asked him along for a walk. "I'm up here for the good of the Family," Massino complained, "and the Family should be taking care of me. But nobody sends me a thing." He said he was especially angry with Bonventre, who was operating out of a social club (Caffe Cesare) on Thirteenth Avenue in Brooklyn, and making a killing selling heroin.

Attanasio understood what the boss was really saying: with Massino in hiding, Bonventre was gaining strength. If Massino did have to go to prison for the murder of the three captains, Bonventre might try to take over the Family. In other words, Massino wanted him dead. The two men wandered back to the house. Before Attanasio and Vitale left, Massino turned to his brother-in-law and issued a direct order. "Whatever Louie tells you to do, do it."

The plot to murder Bonventre would have to be intricate: the Sicilian was a cagey mob veteran who'd be hard to kill. The hit had to be clean, done locally and executed by men Bonventre trusted. Attanasio recruited Vitale and Goldie to work with him. They chose Goldie's chop shop, on a quiet back lane in Maspeth, as the murder location. The trick would be luring the victim inside. Bonventre was too smart to walk into a random meeting—Attanasio's crew needed someone to give him an order he couldn't refuse. That person turned out to be Rusty Rastelli himself. The official boss had just been released from prison, and owed Massino for the three captains' hits. He agreed to summon Bonventre to the Clinton Diner in Maspeth for a supposed meeting. Vitale would pick Bonventre and Attanasio up in a stolen car and chauffeur them to the diner. Out of respect for his captain, Attanasio would let Bonventre ride in the front seat; he would ride in the rear. At the last minute, Vitale would pull onto a road just three blocks away, where the chop shop was located. Goldie, hiding in another car, would radio men in the garage to open the door as the car carrying Bonventre drove by. Attanasio would then shoot Bonventre in the back of the head. In his experience, a bullet to the back of the head "puts them right to sleep." (Louie "HaHa" Attanasio eventually pled guilty to RICO conspiracy charges and was sentenced to fifteen years imprisonment.)

The mob boss, his wife and her brother. It was a love triangle like no other. With Josephine in the gallery and Massino at the defense table, Sal Vitale, the most anticipated witness at the 2004 trial, took his seat in the witness box. The tension was thick: Vitale had been Massino's best friend, lifelong business partner, chief hit man and now, ultimate betrayer. Vitale's testimony was seen as key to the prosecution's case. And he didn't disappoint—his proximity to Massino meant he was able to corroborate practically every charge the Bonanno boss faced. As part of his plea deal, Vitale didn't have to testify against his sister. But she looked on in horror nonetheless as the brother she'd adored explained her husband's life away.

ANDRES: "Now, on the date of the murder of Cesare Bonventre, where were you?"

VITALE: "Driving the car. I went to pick up Louie HaHa and Cesare."

ANDRES: "Where did you pick them up?"

VITALE: "Flushing Avenue and Metropolitan Avenue."

ANDRES: "From the time you picked them up until the time that you got to the garage, can you explain to the jury what happened?"

VITALE: "I pulled up. The car was stolen. It was a car with no console in the center, just a long front seat and a backseat. They get into the car. I start driving toward the location of the garage, only half a mile. When I got to the location, I would have to make a left [into the garage]. I say to Louie HaHa, 'It looks good to me.' That's when he pulled the gun out of his boot and shot him in the back of the head."

ANDRES: "Do you know how many times he shot him?"

VITALE: "One time, and that's when Cesare started fighting me for the steering wheel. I was holding back with my right arm. He was trying to put his foot on the gas pedal to crash the car, as well as trying to grab the wheel. I kept hold of him and that was when Louie HaHa shot him again."

ANDRES: "Where were you going?"

VITALE: "Into the garage, it was open."

ANDRES: "From the time you got into the garage, what happened?"

VITALE: "I jammed on the brakes and jumped out my side. I don't know how, but Cesare ended up on the floor. Louie HaHa was getting out of the backseat, firing at the same time."

The job of flushing Massino out of hiding fell to a fresh-faced agent from Baltimore named Pat Marshall. Marshall became an agent in 1975 after first working as a clerk for the FBI. He spent five years studying nights before landing his spot at the FBI's training academy in Quantico, Virginia. After being transferred to New York, he investigated the Colombo Family and the trigger-happy Jewish Defense League before being assigned to the Bonanno Squad in 1983. By then, Massino had been a fugitive for a year. When Marshall tried to pry information out of his associates, including Sal Vitale, Massino's wife, Josephine, and Linda Lucci, he came up empty-handed. They were all staunchly loyal and said nothing. "We couldn't find him anywhere," Marshall recalled in an interview. "Sal Vitale was a gentleman, but he wasn't going to give us the time of day." Marshall, who has been described as compulsively organized, wouldn't give up. He refused to believe it was hopeless, even if it felt that way.

Then one day, Marshall received an anonymous phone call. The voice told him that every second Friday of the month, Vitale would pull up at Massino's Howard Beach home and load Josephine and the three girls into his car. The caller, who Marshall guessed was a neighbor, was certain Vitale was taking the family to see Massino.

Marshall and his partner set up a stakeout. The next Friday, like clockwork, Vitale arrived at the Massino residence. They tailed the family to a residential street in Brooklyn, and watched as they parked and went inside a row house. At that point, Marshall was certain Massino was inside—why else would the family go to an "unknown location"? The agents sat in their car and waited to see if Massino emerged. "We waited and waited and waited," said Marshall. After more than an hour, they radioed for consent to search and got it.

"I went in the front; my partner went in the back. I knocked on the door. Sal answered. He said, 'Joey's not here but come on in. Look around.' He was very cordial." They found only Josephine and three startled children. Vitale tried hard not to smirk. "We thought we had him," said Marshall. "They knew we didn't. It was disturbing to say the least. We screwed up," he continued. "We should have waited a little longer and taken a road trip to Pennsylvania."

FIVE

A DON IN GOLD CHAINS

On July 14, 1984, Pat Marshall burst into the sunlit foyer of the FBI's Manhattan office tower. The agent had been out in the field with his partner when he got a call saying that there was someone downstairs who needed to be photographed and fingerprinted—someone Marshall would be very interested in seeing. Breathing heavily, Marshall glanced around, not sure who he was looking for. It took only a moment to figure it out. There, as large as life, stood the fugitive who'd eluded him for more than a year. Joseph Massino, the most wanted mobster in America, had entered enemy headquarters on his own free will to surrender. It was the first time Marshall had seen him in the flesh. The forty-year-old

Bonanno captain was standing outside the bulletproof glass entranceway to the FBI's elevator bank, alongside his brother-in-law and wife. He wore a jolly fuck-you expression and a cheap suit.

As awe gave way to nausea, and then to anger, Marshall weaved through the crowd in the direction of his nemesis. He didn't bother to introduce himself. "Get used to my face," he told Massino. "You're gonna see a lot of it."

Earlier that day, Massino had been in another federal officer tower in Lower Manhattan. One St. Andrews Plaza was occupied by New York's two most ambitious prosecutors, Louis Freeh (pronounced "free") and his boss, Southern District U.S. Attorney Rudy Giuliani. Massino and Freeh, head of Giuliani's Oranized Crime Unit, had cut a deal: in return for turning himself in to face charges for conspiracy to murder the three captains, Massino was promised bail. Which meant that after spending twenty months as a fugitive wanted for conspiracy to commit a triple murder, Massino would not set foot in a jail while waiting for his trial to begin. It was a legal triumph for the mobster. He'd always planned to fight the case—if he were to continue to do business in New York, he'd have to. And now that the charges against him had been severed from others accused and convicted of the murders, including Lefty Guns Ruggiero, his chances of acquittal had increased substantially. After the deal was inked, Massino walked freely out of the U.S. Attorney's Office, past the colonnade entranceway of the enormous, neo-classical Federal Courthouse on Foley Square, and into the rear door of the FBI building. He didn't once find himself in custody until Marshall showed up.

"It pissed me off, excuse my French," recalled Marshall of the moment. "You're supposed to work hand in hand with the prosecutors, and Louie Freeh was a former agent. Hey, c'mon, he could've given us a little heads-up." While Freeh took credit for the collar, Marshall was left with a bruised ego and a pile of paperwork. As a mere technicality, he arrested Massino that day in the lobby and took his details, before escorting him downstairs and letting him go.

The 1980s marked a turning point in the government's war against organized crime—and the generals of the battle were rewarded handsomely. Giuliani's mob-busting record got him elected mayor of New York City; in September 1993, President Clinton appointed Freeh director of the FBI. The square-jawed, straight-talking attorney built his profile as a prosecutor, arguing one of the government's most important cases of the era: the 1987 Pizza Connection case. The 1986 Commission Trial was the other great courtroom drama of the decade. Prosecuted by current Homeland Security Secretary Michael Chertoff, it took down four of the five Family dons.

Both the Pizza Connection and Commission cases were fought and won using Giuliani's new atom bomb: the RICO statute. Two FBI agents stumbled across the Racketeer Influenced and Corrupt Organizations Act (RICO) in 1980. Joseph Pistone/Donnie Brasco's contact agent, Jules Bonavolonta, and his colleague, Jim Kossler, attended a lecture given by law professor Robert Blakely at Cornell University in Ithaca, New York. Blakely, who penned the law in 1970, explained to the audience that a single crime—say illegal gambling—could be used as evidence of a pattern to prosecute a criminal enterprise. Kossler and Bonavolonta almost fell off their chairs. Soon after, Giuliani, Freeh and Chertoff had launched RICO into the vernacular as they unmade hundreds of made men, and set about trying to destroy the Five Families. Only one prominent mobster was able to wriggle free of the RICO-wielding prosecutors: none other than Joseph Massino.

In 1987, Massino finally went on trial for conspiracy to murder the three captains. By then, Vitale had been added to the indictment, as had charges for truck hijacking and the murder of cigarette smuggler Dodo Pastore. At the trial, prosecutor Chertoff described Massino as the "Horatio Alger" of the mob. "Violence is not someone you want to invite into your homes for dinner, but he is someone who was embraced by Joe Messina," he said, referring to one of Massino's aliases. Joseph Pistone (Donnie Brasco) also testified against Massino and Vitale. But while a jury had convicted Lefty Ruggiero and his buddies for the triple murder a few years earlier, the jury at the Massino/Vitale trial failed to convict on all counts. Massino and his brother-in-law walked, thanks to a technicality. The spotless records of Freeh and Chertoff had been permanently marred.

Massino did not make it through the eighties unscathed. As he braced to face the three captains case, he was surprised when Pat Marshall arrived at his Howard Beach door waving a separate indictment. Massino was one of thirteen defendants accused of running a giant labor racketeering case involving a union representing the employees of moving companies. Starting in 1964, the Bonannos had used their muscle to stack the leadership of Teamsters Local 814 so they could shake down the city's moving companies: if the movers wanted to do business in the city, they had to pay. The Family also formed a "flying squad" that slashed the tires and burned the trucks of companies that weren't using union workers.

The Bonannos were represented at the Long Island City–based union by a man named Anthony Giliberti, the union vice president. He also happened to be Rusty Rastelli's brother-in-law. After Rastelli got busted in 1975, Massino was given the job of keeping tabs on the union. Once, when Massino thought Giliberti had crossed him, he slapped the union boss across the face. The Chief accused Giliberti of using a thug to set a fire after Massino specifically said he didn't want the man working for the Family. Giliberti vehemently denied the accusation. "You told me not to use him," pleaded Giliberti. "I wouldn't go against you." Massino replied,

"I'll kill you and I'll kill him if I ever find out you were involved in it."

And he meant it. In 1982, when Massino realized the Feds were investigating the union, he dispatched a team of hit men to kill Giliberti, fearing he might flip. Giliberti was shot nine times as he was getting into his car outside his house. But he survived and became the star witness when the union case went to trial in 1986. Rastelli got twelve years and Massino got ten. He would be eligible for parole in five.

Donnie Brasco, the Pizza Connection, Rastelli and Massino behind bars: the Bonanno Family had suffered through a series of devastating blows and had lost its seat on the Commission. Even the FBI was losing interest: in 1987, the Bureau merged two of its La Cosa Nostra crime teams: the Bonanno Squad and the Colombo Squad. For the first time in FBI history, the Bureau did not have a stand-alone crime squad dedicated to each of New York's Five Families. "A lot of Colombos had also been put in jail, and we didn't think we needed a full squad," said Bruce Mouw, who led the joint squad for a brief period in the early nineties.

"For a number of years we had like five or six agents working the Bonannos, which was a big mistake. In the last ten years, we've learned that when these families are down, that's when you jump on them. It's just like warfare. You don't let them regroup five years later. You go out and annihilate them."

The fact was, the Family was only disrupted, not destroyed. They had more than one hundred made members within their ranks, and most of them had escaped the government's crackdown unscathed. The FBI underestimated Massino's ability to run the Family from his cell; he simply passed messages through his visitors to his men on the street, and to other gangs. In the meantime, a new generation loyal to Massino was emerging—men like the new consigliere Anthony Spero, who ran a tough crew from his social club on Bath Avenue, Brooklyn. And, of course, there was Salvatore Vitale, Massino's right-hand man and the acting boss during Massino's five-year stint in prison. If there was anyone who could manage the Family in the boss's absence, it was Good-Looking Sal.

Joey Massino and Sal Vitale had been buddies since childhood. They grew up in the same part of Queens and went to the same high school. Vitale had three sisters; Massino began dating Josephine Vitale, or "Josie," as she was known at home, when she was just sixteen. He became a fixture in the Vitale household, and was like the brother Sal Vitale never had.

In the late sixties, Vitale returned home from Germany, where he'd been stationed as a paratrooper in the Army, and went to work for his old friend. By then, Massino and Josephine had three young daughters and were running their lunch wagon business out of J&J Catering in Maspeth. When he was about twenty years old, Vitale bought a truck and route from his brother-in-law for sixteen thousand dollars. He ran numbers from his wagon, and helped unload stolen trucks. By the early seventies, he had started doing breaking-and-entering crimes on the side with two of Massino's other drivers. One day, he returned to Massino's deli to unload his wagon when the big man pulled him to the side. "I heard you're doing scoring," said Massino. Vitale said he wasn't, but the boss knew better. "Don't lie to me," said Massino, "Phil Rastelli sent me the word." Massino didn't have a problem with Vitale stealing—it was just the fact that he wasn't in on it that bothered him. "If you're going to do scores," Massino continued, "do them with me." From then on, Vitale was no longer just a brother-in-law, friend and part-time employee—he belonged to Massino. He had to clear every crime with the chief, and give him a cut of all his earnings.

Sal Vitale was always a clever criminal. Around the time that he started working full-time for Massino, he got a tip about a cold storage warehouse full of fur pelts from a friend who operated an elevator in Manhattan's fur district. Vitale promptly posed as a fur dealer and rented a cage in the warehouse—which had over fifty cages filled with valuable pelts—under a false name. The brilliance of the plan was that he knew the fur dealers wouldn't notice they were missing pelts right away. In August, when fur sales are at their lowest, the dealers take their summer vacations. So when the end of the summer rolled around, Vitale, wearing a fake beard, and Goldie, with his hair dyed dark brown, slipped into the warehouse, cut through the cages belonging to dealers, removed the pelts and put them in their own cage. They waited a couple of days, then returned to the warehouse, walked right in and removed the furs from their cage as if they owned them. Another time, he and Big Louie Tartaglione torched a dentist's office in Hamilton Place, Queens. The dentist was a friend of Massino's and wanted the insurance money. Vitale and Big Louie placed three containers of gasoline, each with a rope tied around the top, around the office. They lit a small, contained fire in the center of the room; when they got outside, they pulled the ropes to make the containers fall over. The office went up in flames.

Arson and robbery were among the many cowboy crimes Vitale pulled off in the seventies and eighties. He became such a capable and prolific criminal that Massino made him his second-in-command—the drill sergeant under General Massino. Vitale took care of the day-to-day affairs, leaving Massino time to plan strategy and think about the bigger picture. Massino personally handed over his prized sports-betting operation to Vitale, and often had him organize the men when a load of swag came in.

The Chief trusted Vitale to get the job done and keep his mouth shut, and Vitale loved him for it. He deeply respected his brother-in-law, and did anything he asked. He drove Massino to meetings with Family bosses in Little Italy; he acted as a buffer between

Massino and the men. When it came to organizing hits, Vitale was total pro. When Massino gave the order, he knew he could count on Vitale to make it happen.

Sal Vitale wasn't good-looking by the time he reached the courtroom. His dark coloring and sharp facial structure, which earned him his nickname, had been replaced by gray hair and sagging features—it must be true that "The Life" prematurely ages you. But on the stand, Vitale's mind was as quick as the day he joined up. His memories of crimes committed on Massino's watch were as comprehensive as they were devastating.

ANDRES: "Were you ever responsible for running the Bonanno Family?"

VITALE: "Yes, I was."

ANDRES: "Over what period of time were you responsible for running the Bonanno Family?"

VITALE: "Late eighties, until '93. Until Joe came home."

ANDRES: "Where was he?"

VITALE: "Incarcerated."

ANDRES: "Do you know where he was incarcerated?"

VITALE: "Talladega, Alabama."

ANDRES: "During the time that you were responsible for running the Bonanno Family, were you responsible for doing it alone or with somebody else?"

VITALE: "Anthony Spero."

ANDRES: "Who was Anthony Spero?"

VITALE: "My consigliere."

ANDRES: "Do you know who appointed Anthony Spero as consigliere of the Bonanno Family?"

VITALE: "Yes, Joe Massino."

ANDRES: "You testified that Mr. Massino was in prison. Did you ever visit him?"

VITALE: "Yes, I did."

ANDRES: "What prisons did you visit him in?"

VITALE: "Visited him once or twice in Otisville [Upstate New York]. Numerous times at the MCC Manhattan, and Talladega, Alabama."

ANDRES: "And how often did you visit Mr. Massino in Alabama?"

VITALE: "Once a month."

ANDRES: "Prior to the time that Mr. Massino went to prison, did he give you and Anthony Spero any instructions about how you were supposed to run the Bonanno Family?"

VITALE: "He told us we couldn't break any captains, we couldn't transfer any money, couldn't make any men."

ANDRES: "Did he tell you anything about what power you would have in terms of murders?"

VITALE: "Only to defend ourselves at all costs."

Vitale took to wearing tailored suits after he became the Family's acting boss during Massino's incarceration. He preferred dark, distinguished ones with wide lapels and sharp lines. He set them off with silk ties and matching handkerchiefs, folded and tucked into the top pocket of his coat. The new don donned a large gold ring on the third finger of his left hand, which went nicely with the heavy link bracelet he wore on his right wrist. Massino was behind iron bars, and Vitale was in gold chains. In the seventies, he played chauffeur; in the eighties, he cleaned up after hits. Now, in the nineties, he was running one of the great Mafia Families. He gave the commands. He ordered the hits, and he was making most of the money. Having been elevated to the top slot by default, Vitale suddenly learned how good it was to be in charge.

Vitale frequented a new social club in the mid-eighties. Until then, he'd been the "S" behind the "J" at the discreet J&S Cake. But Vitale's new club was located prominently on Grand Avenue, Maspeth's main drag, right next door to the local branch of the Queens Borough Library. Massino had designated Tuesday as the night when the Family gathered at his club, but Vitale made a point of being different: he had the men come on Thursdays. He wanted to be his own man. But in his haste to enrich himself, Vitale lacked what came naturally to Massino: the ability to lead and the respect of his followers.

Money is what drives the Mafia, and perhaps the most consistent way of generating it is through gambling—a fact not lost on the Bonannos or the money-hungry Vitale. One common gambling enterprise is Joker Poker, played for 25 cents a pop on slot-like machines in pizza parlors and neighborhood dive bars across New York City. Instead of spinning wheels of fruit, each game deals a five-card hand of poker. Winning hands are rewarded with credits, which can be cashed in at any time. Of course, the odds are stacked heavily in the computer's favor: a single machine can generate up to $15,000 a week.

Bootsie Tomasulo, a Bonanno soldier, had a gigantic Joker Poker fleet. He owned so many machines, he had trouble collecting all the money that was poured into them. His son Anthony made the rounds each week, opening the machines with a key and sticking a pin into a keyhole, which lit up on the screen the number of quarters the game had swallowed since the last time he checked. Then he'd settle up with the storekeeper or bar manager, who got 50 percent of the takings in return.

One day, while sitting peacefully on his stoop, Bootsie had an asthma attack and died. After he was buried with full Mafia honors, the question was raised as to who would inherit his electronic empire. His son Anthony naturally believed it was his right to carry on his collecting the money, but Sal Vitale conveniently put the Family ahead of the family. The new acting boss maintained that when a wiseguy died, his rackets reverted to the boss—after all, it was the boss who protected the rackets in the first place. In other words, Bootsie's Joker Poker business would go to Vitale alone.

Vitale had his man Mickey Cardello break the news to Anthony Tomasulo, who was none too pleased. He could hardly sue, so he did what gangsters do best: he threatened to hurt people. "If I have to, I'll kill you and I'll kill Sal," Tomasulo screamed at Cardello. Tomasulo was so angry he repeated the threat to another Bonanno captain, and even said he was going to take the dispute to Vincent "The Chin" Gigante, Massino's old foe, the Genovese Family boss. But all he was doing was writing his own death sentence. Vitale wasn't about to risk it all over an upstart kid—he decided to kill the young Tomasulo before things got out of hand. Vitale went to see consigliere Anthony Spero to make it official. "You better do it," said Spero. "Get it behind you. God forbid he kills you. We'll all lose." Like magic, Anthony Tomasulo vanished, and Vitale hit the jackpot.

Salvatore Vitale had four children, all of them boys. Massino often pressed his men to recruit their sons into the Family, but Vitale wanted a better life for his sons. He and his wife raised them in Long Island, a safe distance from Mafia City. Of course, they still caused him no end of trouble, and even though he didn't press them in to the family business, he didn't spare them his temper, as one exchange with Assistant U.S. Attorney Greg Andres showed.

ANDRES: "During the time in the 1990s, did you have a son who worked in the *New York Post*?"

VITALE: "Yes."

ANDRES: "What did he do there?"

VITALE: "Not much."

ANDRES: "How did you know that?"

VITALE: "I was at breakfast with Bobby Perrino (a supervisor in the distribution arm of the *Post*) in a bagel store and asked how my son was doing. He says, 'Doing okay.' 'What does my son do?' I asked. He says, 'Your son doesn't do anything.' 'My son doesn't do anything? I want you to have him working, maybe he'll go back to college. I thought you were doing me a favor. You are not doing me a favor.' I went home and questioned my son. 'What do you do at the *New York Post*?' He said, 'I don't do nothing.' 'You are fired, don't go back there again.' From that point on, he was fired."

ANDRES: "How was it you had the authority to fire him from the *New York Post*?"

VITALE: "Because I flew over the coffee table and

strangled him on the couch (and said) 'Don't go back to the *Post*.'"

Vitale's boy wasn't the only person connected to the Bonannos who "did nothing" at the *New York Post* in that era. In the early nineties, the Family had its hooks deeply embedded in the distribution arm of the newspaper, then located on Manhattan's Lower East Side. There, in the wee hours of the morning, the ink-smudged building buzzed with conveyer belts and forklifts as workers went about delivering close to 500,000 papers each day. The operations required an army of men to bundle the papers as they came off the press, and a fleet of truck drivers to deliver the bundles to bodegas across the five boroughs.

The Bonannos' newspaper racket was a classic, albeit brazen, organized labor scheme. For starters, the labor pool was infested with wiseguys, including three made members of the Family. The Bonannos were paid the wages—some of which amounted to $50,000 a year—of no less than fifty-one no-show employees. In addition to the labor scam, sweetheart contracts went to friends of the Family, who kicked some money back as a way of returning the favor. And for years, Family members stole thousands of papers a day and sold them to vendors for twenty to thirty cents each (they were then fifty cents). The Bonannos became so entrenched at the *Post* they ran loan-sharking operations, sold guns and planned drug deals right out of the building.

But while the Bonannos were growing rich and complacent, the New York State police quietly began probing Mafia infiltration of the newspaper industry. None of the city's mastheads was found to be as crime-ridden as the *Post*. As the investigation heated up, the police hid a bug in the office of Robert Perrino, the same delivery superintendent who employed Vitale's son. Perrino happened to be the son of former Family underboss Nicolas "Nicky Glasses" Marangello, who'd operated out of the notorious Toyland social club in Little Italy. Perrino wasn't a made member of the Family, but he did run the distribution arm of the *Post* and doubled as the Bonannos' front man. And he had his hands practically wedged in the cash register—it was Perrino who dished out all the no-show jobs, and Perrino who doctored the books so that the stolen paper bundles were never missed. He even did a little shylocking on the side. Perrino was also in constant contact with Vitale, and personally handed him six hundred dollars in tribute money every week.

When the law finally came down on the *Post*'s crooked workforce, and Perrino was arrested along with twelve other Bonannos, Vitale got nervous. Although he hadn't been named in the initial indictments, he knew things could change in an instant—all it would take were one man's flapping gums. Vitale was directly linked to the *Post* racket through Perrino, and Perrino was facing serious charges. It was Perrino's office that had been bugged, and Sal feared his name might have been caught on tape. And since Perrino wasn't a made member, he was less likely to do time to protect the Family. Surely the Feds would offer him a way out if he sang, thought Vitale. With Massino in prison, there was no way Sal Vitale was going to give up the power and trappings afforded to a Mafia boss without a fight.

Vitale's first move was to contact another Bonanno who worked at the *Post*, Richard Cantarella. He was listed as a "tail man"—a worker who rides on the back of the delivery truck and unloads the bundles— but in fact he paid a laborer twenty dollars a night to do the work while he collected seven hundred dollars a week. Vitale knew Cantarella could get close to Perrino without arousing suspicion. He arranged to meet Cantarella at a hotel to discuss the problem. Once there, he led them down to the pool area, where the sound of running water would muffle anything that could be picked up on a microphone. Vitale asked, "Is Bobby Perrino showing signs of weakness?" Cantarella was a dangerous man, so he knew exactly what Vitale was getting at. But he was cautious in his reply. "I don't see him that often, very seldom," he said, "but last time we spoke, he didn't show any signs of weakness I could see."

It didn't matter. Vitale had already made up his mind: he wanted Perrino dead.

Sal Vitale's next visit was to Anthony Spero—as Massino's consigliere, Spero had to have a hand in every decision to carry out a murder. The two men met in a diner near Spero's Bath Avenue club. The conversation Vitale had with his partner was very different from the one he'd had with Cantarella; in fact, he told Spero that it was Cantarella who'd voiced concerns about Perrino, and that it was Cantarella who wanted him dead. "Bobby Perrino will never stand up to the pressure," he claimed Cantarella said. After Vitale had finished posturing, Spero made the only logical conclusion he could: Perrino had to go.

The next week, Anthony Perrino failed to show up for work. His body remained hidden until December 2003, when his skeleton was found embedded in the concrete floor of a construction company in Staten Island. He'd been shot multiple times in the head. The government was denied their star witness, and besides a handful of Bonannos who were sent briefly to Rikers Island, the Family escaped largely unscathed.

Phil Rastelli died in 1991, and was buried in a cemetery in Maspeth. The wake, held a few blocks down the road at the Grand Avenue club, lasted for three days. Every made guy in the Family attended. The FBI came along too—agents openly photographed the event. They understood it was a landmark moment for the Bonannos. With Rastelli gone, the Family needed to crown a new official leader. The choice was obvious: Joseph Massino had been running the Family since the murder of the three captains ten years before.

There was something almost sentimental about the passing of the torch from Rastelli to Massino. Unlike

John Gotti, who had his boss Paul Castellano gunned down in public, Massino had waited patiently for Rastelli to die of natural causes—an unusual event for a mob boss. Despite prompting from captains who believed the ailing Rastelli was weak, Massino refused to hurry Rastelli's passing. He'd earned the right to be boss, and he wanted it to be official. But when the moment came, Massino wasted no time: he sent word to Vitale from prison to have Spero call a meeting of the captains. (As consigliere, it was appropriate that Spero make the first move.) According to Massino's instructions, Vitale was to nominate him as boss at the meeting, and loyal soldier James "Big Louie" Tartaglione was, if necessary, to second it. After Rastelli had been laid to rest, that's exactly what happened: Massino was unanimously elected boss of the Family. The kid who'd dropped out of school in eighth grade and whose sole vocational qualification was a license to drive lunch wagons was now officially in charge. He answered to no one. There was nothing he couldn't do.

Directly across the street from the social club on Grand Avenue was a two-story building with a small diner on the street level. On the second level of the building was an old dentist's suite, which hadn't been used for years—at least, not for anything having to do with teeth. But that didn't mean it wasn't alive with activity. As Maspeth's residents strolled past the old place, they failed to notice that, each afternoon, the venetian blinds hanging in the second-story windows slowly parted, and then closed again in the early evening. Every so often, a man slipped in the side entrance with a stack of pizza boxes or brown paper bags stuffed with sandwiches.

The people who went into the old dentist's office spent most of their time watching television, but they only ever watched one program: *The Vitale Show*. Unbeknownst to Vitale or his cronies across the street was the fact that the FBI was viewing their every move. In the early nineties, the bureau secured a Title 3 warrant allowing it to install a hidden camera in the wall of the club. The technical experts also wired the club for sound. The result was a crystal-clear black-and-white closed-circuit TV picture, which was aired in real time around the clock to up to ten agents, for eight months straight.

The FBI stumbled on the club during a routine surveillance operation in the late eighties, when agents tailed a Bonanno man, Louie Restivo, to Grand Avenue. The Bureau promptly rented the old dental space and set up a roster of lensmen who captured almost every Bonanno captain coming and going over the next year and a half. "You had to be careful about what time it was," recalled FBI agent Jack Stubing. "If you had lights on behind you, they'd be able to see what you were doing." Hence, explained Stubing, the elaborate venetian blind routine.

But it was worth the trouble: Lino was a candid camera standout, often wearing loud sweaters pulled tight over his portly frame. Goldie was also very photogenic, striking a cool pose in one shot, leaning casually against the front gate, talking, in a pair of dark sunglasses. But the real keeper was a snapshot of Vitale wearing a white shirt with the top three buttons undone, exposing his chest. His gelled hair sparkled in the sunshine as he gestured to his left. Spero was also in the frame, but in contrast to the dapper don wannabe, he was wearing a mangy velour sweat suit with what looked like the remains of his lunch down the front.

As part of the operation, the FBI also installed listening devices outside the club. The Bonannos were too security-conscious to discuss business inside, so they would take walk-talks up and down Grand Avenue. Stubing said: "The participants in the conversation would walk up and down the street, and someone would follow along behind to make sure no one was following along behind, trying to listen in." But the wiseguys weren't as wise as they could have been: there was one spot in the concrete backyard of the club where they often lingered as they talked shop. The FBI had put a bug in that exact spot.

Eventually, the government accumulated enough evidence to stage a raid. In June 1992, Stubing and a team of agents carrying shotguns paid the Bonannos a visit. When they burst inside the club, they found Vitale seated at one end of a long rectangular table, flanked by eighteen of his senior aides. The agents told the Bonannos to stay exactly where they were, to put their hands on the table where they could be seen, and to say "cheese." The snapshot is famous within the small circle of New York's mob sleuths, and is commonly known as the "Last Supper" photo. No one can remember a time when so many senior-ranking Mafia men were caught meeting in one place at one time.

Afterward, the Feds rounded up nine Bonannos on a string on loan-sharking and illegal sports betting charges in a case known as "Grand Finale." Mickey Cardello, who was named a decade later in the flurry of indictments before Massino's trial, faced the most serious charges. He had been recorded proudly giving what Stubing calls the "One day this will all be yours speech" to his son. "He was saying words to the effect of, 'We are building something great and things are going so well that we soon won't be able to hide all the money.'" But despite the fabulous audiovisuals, the case never went to trial. Every one of the accused Bonannos pleaded guilty and served a range of minor sentences. The Bonanno Squad never got a shot of a body being rolled up in a carpet, or a tape of anyone describing a homicide. Vitale himself was never once intercepted on a wire and was never named in the indictment. In the absence of those items, the FBI needed one thing: a rat. But not a single Bonanno man talked.

On Friday, November 13, 1992, Joseph Massino—the newly crowned official boss of the Bonanno Crime Family—was released from prison.

SIX

THE GHOST

Just inside the door of the CasaBlanca restaurant was a board covered in snapshots of movie stars who had dropped in for dinner. They include James Caan (*The Godfather*), Johnny Depp (*Donnie Brasco*) and Hugh Grant (*Mickey Blue Eyes*), arm-in-arm with Elizabeth Hurley. At first glance, the place seemed an unlikely hot spot for celebrities—it looked more like a factory than a restaurant. The square, yellow-brick building was located on a grubby street corner in a run-down, semi-industrial neighborhood in Maspeth, Queens. A red neon sign in the window read PASTA, and its maroon awnings were emblazoned on all sides with the word *catering*. Inside, the place was pure Italianate kitsch, complete with neon-lined arches, walls deco-rated with bronze-tinted mirrors, and plastic flowers sitting on brass stands in corners.

But the actors didn't come to CasaBlanca for the food, or the ambiance. They came because, as the menu announced on the front, it was "CasaBlanca: Where You Are Part of the Family!" The family, in this case, *was* headed by Joseph Massino. CasaBlanca was Massino's haunt, personal refrigerator and base of operation. And it was here, among plastic flowers and meatball subs, that Massino orchestrated the most successful Mafia comeback in living memory.

I dined at CasaBlanca one evening in 2003. When I walked in, I saw five men in crumpled suits sitting at a round table having a raucous good time. They turned quiet and suspicious when my friend and I were led to our table. They were undoubtedly "connected," and perhaps one or two were actually made. Next to the main group of characters, at a second table, sat another two men who wore velour sweat suits. I guessed they were drivers or bodyguards.

After the initial unease of our arrival, a tuxedo-wearing waiter took my wine order and returned with a bottle of red. Moments after he filled my glass, I spilled the bright liquid right across the white linen tablecloth. The waiter smiled and told me it was good luck. I was going to need it.

Besides the regulars and us, the place was empty—it seemed like more of a private club than a restaurant. Trying hard to hide my nerves, I glanced around and spied two gray metal objects shaped like shoeboxes bolted to the ceiling, above where the main group sat. Both boxes had black rubber knobs, which appeared to be aerials, poking out from their ends. Though I couldn't prove it, my hunch was they were Bearcat scanners: electronic devices used to detect frequency transmissions. In other words, had anyone been wearing a transmitter, the Bearcats would have picked up the signal and echoed our conversation back through the restaurant's sound system. We'd all have known who the rat was among us.

My meal with the mob occurred six months after Massino was arrested for the last time. But it was obvious that, throughout his legal tribulations, CasaBlanca remained a Bonanno stronghold. It was run by the made guy Louie Restivo.

Massino opened CasaBlanca after he got off parole, when he began his rise to absolute power. Each of his captains patronized the restaurant at least once a month—his favorites came every week. But they weren't coming to talk business. Except for the occasional whisper in the catering hall, there was a hard-and-fast rule that if you needed to "talk" about something, you took a walk-talk around the block. No, the Bonannos who came to CasaBlanca did so purely to show their faces and pay respect. Massino was now the Family's official boss, and as such deserved the formal displays of deference. When they walked into the restaurant, they would approach their leader first, kiss him on both cheeks and slip a fat envelope of greenbacks into his hand. Massino was the man, or as they said, "The man in the white house."

At trial, Massino's defense attorney didn't deny that his client was the Bonanno boss—he just insisted it wasn't a crime, and that Massino was a benevolent despot who never hurt anyone. But when prosecutor Greg Andres asked Salvatore Vitale to testify to Massino's role, the jury heard a different story.

ANDRES: "What is the scope the authority the boss of an organized crime family has?"

VITALE: "He has absolute power."

ANDRES: "You testified earlier that Mr. Massino was surveillance conscious. Was there ever a time when Mr. Massino was referred to by a specific gesture?"

VITALE: "Yes. Touching your ear."

ANDRES: "Who instructed you to do that and why?"

VITALE: "He did, so we wouldn't get his name on tape. If you talk to an individual, just in case he was wired."

JUDGE GARAUFIS: "Let the record reflect that the witness touched his ear with his hand when he made that statement."

ANDRES: "With respect to the time that Mr. Massino told you to refer to him by touching your ear, when was that?"

VITALE: "Right after he got out of jail."

ANDRES: "What is the roll of underboss in an organized crime family?"

VITALE: "The role of the underboss is to say yes to the boss, to take out the orders to the men, to be a buffer for the boss. The boss is not really supposed to meet with the men. He's beyond that. It is your job to meet with the men and bring the messages forward."

ANDRES: "You say, act as a buffer. What does that mean?"

VITALE: "To insulate him from the captains, to protect him."

ANDRES: "Why would it be a problem if the boss were meeting directly with the captains?"

VITALE: "Number one, it would give the boss more time to think about the situation, so he had time to think which way he wanted to go. Number two, he's beyond that. Why should he sit with a captain? The captain could be wired, an informant. It's for many reasons. He picks and chooses who he wants to sit with."

ANDRES: "Is it important in organized crime for the members, the captains, of the Bonanno Family, to protect the boss?"

VITALE: "At all costs."

ANDRES: "Why is that?"

VITALE: "You are only as strong as your boss. You are only as strong as your boss to the other Families."

Joe Massino knew he had work to do after he got out of jail in 1992. On top of the agenda was reforming his organization. The FBI was as dogged as ever, and the other Families were still fierce competitors in New York's criminal marketplace. There were only so many ways to make an illegal buck, and Massino wanted to be involved in as many as possible. With the eighties still fresh in his mind, and the smell of prison still in his nostrils, Massino realized he had to change the way he did business if the Family were to rebuild and survive.

Ironically, the Donnie Brasco episode had, in some ways, started the job. After being booted from the Commission, the Bonannos became organized crime's pariah, and were forced to diversify. For example, they were one of the first Families to exploit the stock market. In the meantime, the other four Families remained involved in high-profit, high-risk enterprises like labor racketeering, carving up the city's colossal construction industry between them. The famous 1991 "Windows Case"—a giant bid-rigging and extortion scheme that brought in a two-dollar mob tax for every window installed by the New York Housing Authority—involved every crime gang but the Bonannos. And when the legendary mob turncoats Sammy "The Bull" Gravano, underboss of the Gambinos, and Alphonse "Little Al" D'Arco, underboss of the Luccheses, cooperated with the FBI, they had nothing on Massino's men.

As Massino rebuilt traditional rackets like extortion, loan-sharking and sports betting, he stayed away from anything that would expose the Bonannos. As the newly liberated Family grew stronger and stronger, they realized they liked operating alone. In the mid-nineties, several Families proposed forming a joint committee to deal with construction unions. One representative from each Family would sit on it. But Massino wasn't interested: "We've never had nothing to do with construction," he said at the time. "What are we doing here? We're only going to have a problem for no reason whatsoever. Let's just forget about it."

Massino also tinkered with the Family's internal structures to insulate and protect it from itself. He was furious with Vitale for the surveillance fiasco at the Grand Avenue club. No longer would the Bonannos assemble en masse—Masssino ordered the crews to shutter all the clubs. If the men had to meet, they would do so in run-down diners or vacant lots, and never in the same place twice. He instructed his captains to have nothing to do with one another. The crews were split into cells; the soldiers in respective regimes; they were told they weren't allowed to associate. That way, if an informant or undercover agent infiltrated a crew, they wouldn't be able to reveal (wittingly or unwittingly) information about the rest of the Family.

For his part, Massino stopped going to weddings and wakes—by then, every Family function had FBI photographers outside collecting enterprise evidence for potential RICO trials. Massino decreed that only one representative from each crew could go; that representative would carry an envelope from each man who stayed home. Massino also encouraged his men to nominate their sons for membership, reasoning that blood relatives wouldn't rat out their own. He wanted the Family as tight-knit as possible. He outlawed the use of guns and knives at initiation ceremonies. If the place were raided, the cops would instantly recognize the props and use them as evidence.

Massino realized that arrests were inevitable no matter how tight he turned the screws. So to fight the

Feds, he built a war chest to pay legal bills. As part of the privilege of being a member of his Family, money would be given to wiseguys who couldn't afford an attorney when they were arrested. Each month, every member of the Family was required to chip in one hundred dollars to the chest. Also as part of the new deal, Massino made his men vow never to speak to law enforcement officials, even in passing. He didn't want anyone getting too friendly with the neighborhood agent or local beat cop. If they were approached by the FBI, they were to turn around and walk away.

One of the most important changes Massino made was to set up a new chain of command. A year after he got out a prison, he met secretly with a core group of his most trusted lieutenants. As he was still on parole, he was strictly forbidden from associating with known criminals, so the meeting was held in a warehouse. The men attending didn't know they'd be seeing Massino until he walked into the room. After bear hugs and cheek kisses all around, he told them he was happy to see them and wanted to know everything. How was business? How was the morale of the men? Did they have gripes? What did they need from him? After five years behind bars, he wanted to know every single detail about his Family, and to tell his plans.

"I'm thinking of putting a committee together," Massino said. "I think that's the way to go." Made up of senior members who made decisions and settled disputes on the boss's behalf, committees weren't a new concept, but were usually formed when the boss was in prison. But Massino realized there was an advantage to allowing his top men to run the show: he would be free to make policy and, more important, would stay clean. He wanted nothing to do with the day-to-day headaches and risks of running the show. The videotapes of his friend John Gotti giving orders at his Little Italy club, the Ravenite, were being played over and over at mob trials to show the kowtowing afforded to a mob boss. Massino learned from Gotti's mistakes. The committee, not the boss, would give the orders to the captains. If the men had a problem, they would tell the committee. As such, the committee would put a barrier between him and the Family. No one besides a handful of Massino's most trusted would speak to him or see him. The captains wouldn't even be given Massino's phone number.

From that point on, Massino rarely went out in public. He left his Howard Beach home only to go to CasaBlanca or to drive out to a commercial kitchen he part-owned in Long Island. The Family rank and file had been isolated from one another, and he from them. Eventually, they ceased speaking his name entirely, referring to him only with a tug of the ear. Massino was there, but not there: an ever-present entity who never actually materialized. He was an enigma, a mystery, a ghost of a man almost completely unknown to the public. He had no interest in making the papers—the FBI and the Justice Department weren't going to feel as much political pressure to take him down if the media didn't create it. The only flash of ego Massino let slip as he painstakingly rebuilt the Family was giving it his name. Vitale was dispatched to quietly spread the word: they were no longer to be known for the traitor Joseph Bonanno. The Family was to take the name of the new boss. For the first time in forty years, one of New York's Five Families had a new title: the Massino Family. (To this day, the media as well as law enforcement continue to refer to the Family by its old name, Bonanno, but in the underworld, the name Massino carried more weight.)

* * *

As he lingered in the shadows, New York's other bosses stole the front page: the heads of the Gambino (Peter Gotti), Lucchese (Vic Amuso), Genovese (Vincent Gigante) and Colombo (Carmine Persico) families were all either doing hard time or waiting to stand trial. Being the sole operating New York boss gave Massino a kind of moral advantage over the other families, and he consolidated his right of might with one master stroke.

Massino called a meeting of the Mafia Commission, the first in years. It was held at the home of his CasaBlanca partner, Louie Restivo, and drew top men from the other families, including two consiglieres and two acting bosses. The conversation meandered around topics like the still-smoldering Colombo War and a dispute over rights to the parking garage leases at Staten Island University Hospital. But Massino soon took charge. He had the big picture on his mind: he argued that the core values of the mob were being eroded. There was no stock taken in the old traditions of trust and honor, which had kept them strong for so long. Their ranks were lousy with drug dealers and informants. Massino proposed that from that day forward, only full-blooded Italians could be made. It wasn't enough to have, say, an Italian father and an Irish mother. It was vital to keep the mob's blood pure so that the extended family remained tight-knit and interdependent. He also forcefully argued that tougher penalties be meted out to drug offenders. If apprehended, major drug dealers often faced sentences like those of murderers, and were more likely to flip. At Massino's urging, the Commission ruled that anyone connected to a family who'd been sent to prison for drug dealing would have to wait at least five years before they could be nominated for full-time membership. This time around, Massino wasn't going to let anything—or anyone—get in his way.

Every Monday and Thursday, Massino would drive out to a business called King Catering, a commercial kitchen in Farmingdale, Long Island. It was one of Massino's favorite haunts, and the place where he indulged his love of the culinary arts—he went there to while away the hours, preparing himself heaping helpings of pasta and sauce. When he wasn't cooking in the kitchen, he was playing cards or cracking jokes with Tommy and Kevin, the two owners. But Massino wasn't just there to hang with the guys. For his two days a week, he got paid eight thousand dollars a month. In mob-speak, the arrangement Massino had with the owners is what's known as "protection."

Of course, the concept of protection had been the bread and butter of the Italian American Mafia for more than a hundred years. The early twentieth-century gangsters who patrolled Little Italy's tenement slums famously received protection money from local storekeepers as payment for policing the neighborhood, scaring away other criminals who'd otherwise shake them down. It was a lose-lose situation: if the store owners didn't pay, they'd be beaten, burned or worse by the Family enforcers. The lesser of two evils was as good as it got in 1910, as well as in 1993.

Massino's version wasn't quite so confrontational. In fact, according to testimony, it was the owners of King Catering who came to him. There was another large commercial kitchen six exits up off the Expressway, which happened to be operated by a member of the Lucchese Family named Carmine Avellino. Avellino was a nasty customer who would later be convicted of killing a garbage hauler. Naturally, he was none too pleased about the competition he was getting from the boys who dared to cross him at King Catering. Given his reputation, Tommy and Kevin realized they had a serious problem—forget losing business, they might actually end up dead. In other words, they needed protection.

King Catering reached out to Massino and Vitale, who agreed to meet with Avellino and make clear that the business he was threatening was "theirs." They held the sit-down at the Little Italy social club of then-Bonanno underboss Stevie Beef. Massino, Beef and Carmine Avellino sat at one table while Vitale and Avellino's brother, Sal, sat at a side table nearby. During the sit-down, Beef told Carmine that the owner of King Catering was a distant relative and the business "belonged" to the Bonanno Family, and that the Luccheses were not to touch it. It was a bold-faced lie—Beef had never so much as met the owners—but it worked. From that point on, King Catering didn't have any more problems.

Not long after, Massino and Vitale became the proud new partners of King Catering. Tommy and Kevin drove out to J&S Cake to hammer out the nuts and bolts of the new arrangement. To prevent prying questions from the FBI or the IRS, they would have to make the partnership "official": Massino and Vitale agreed to give the owners twenty-five thousand dollars each year for three years, at which time the pair would become legal partners. Contracts were drawn up that said Massino and Vitale were in charge of "packing." Aside from fixing the ice machine one time, the pair never did a scrap of work, and for their seventy-five grand they got a third of a company that was bringing in millions. They went so far as to set up a front company called Queens Catering into which their protection money was paid. On paper, Queens Catering appeared so upstanding that Massino and Vitale used the company kitty to pay their family BlueCross BlueShield health insurance. In the end, Massino and Vitale sold their share of King Catering back to Tommy and Kevin for $650,000, more than eight times what they had paid to get it.

Vitale spoke in a matter-of-fact monotone, dulling the jury's senses. He described murder after murder with the same attitude an exterminator might take to killing roaches: if they annoy you, get rid of them. Simple. But even Vitale's testimony had its lighter moments.

ANDRES: "Mr. Vitale, I was asking you questions about King Catering. During the course of your involvement with Mr. Massino and King Catering, did you ever discuss with him any alibi he would use if he got arrested or got in trouble for King Catering?"

VITALE: "Yes. He said he made the sauce, and the sauce was very important."

ANDRES: "I am sorry?"

VITALE: "He said he made the sauce for King Catering, and sauce is very important."

ANDRES: "He said that he made the sauce?"

VITALE: "Sauce."

ANDRES: "He said that he actually made the sauce or is that what he would say if he was arrested?"

VITALE: "He made the sauce one time."

ANDRES: "Did you have a discussion about his defense and what he would say about King Catering if he was ever arrested for it?"

VITALE: "He said his defense would be that he made the sauce, and the sauce was very important."

ANDRES: "During the course of the time, more than fifteen years, that you were associated with King Catering, do you know if Mr. Massino ever made the sauce there?"

VITALE: "Maybe once or twice."

ANDRES: "During the time that Mr. Massino was

incarcerated, would he ever talk to you about the sauce at King Catering?"

VITALE: "No."

Everything was going according to plan. Massino's new regime had made the Family stronger and more impenetrable than ever before. The money was flowing in, in seemingly endless amounts. The other New York families were affording him a new level of respect. Joe Massino had only one task left in order to take total control—only one last threat to get rid of.

Salvatore Vitale.

Massino didn't like the way Vitale had run the Family while he was in prison. The word from the trenches was Good Looking Sal was an arrogant liar, despised by men who privately said he'd abused his power while Massino was in jail. They whispered that Vitale had killed Robert Perrino, the supervisor at the *Post,* and others for the good of himself, not the good of the Family. Vitale had grown arrogant and power-hungry during his time as acting boss, and Massino had reason to think he had aspirations of keeping the job for good. Massino wasn't blind—the Colombo War began when

Carmine "Junior" Persico, while serving life in prison tried to demote his acting boss and install his son, Alphonse, in his place. Joey Massino wasn't about to make the same mistake.

But the Bonanno boss knew he couldn't just kill his brother-in-law. Instead, he borrowed a strategy from Michael Corleone in *The Godfather*: he kept his friends close, but his enemies closer. And he did it in a creative way. In order to foil any leadership aspirations Vitale might have had, Massino officially made him second in command. During a ceremony, he and Vitale locked hands and Massino named him underboss. But in the context of Massino's new committee, the move severed, rather than boosted, Vitale's power. He no longer had any muscle on the street; he wasn't a captain, nor did he have many supporters. All of his former responsibilities had been delegated to the committee. All of a sudden, Vitale was isolated and alone. He had nothing left but an empty title.

ANDRES: "You testified about Joseph Massino. Can you explain to the jury how you first met Joseph Massino?"

VITALE: "I met him through my sister."

ANDRES: "How old were you at the time?"

VITALE: "I would say eleven or twelve."

ANDRES: "Can you describe the nature of your relationship with him?"

VITALE: "It was a good relationship."

ANDRES: "Did you become close?"

VITALE: "Yes."

ANDRES: "Did you spend much time with Mr. Massino?"

VITALE: "When I bought my catering truck, I would see him on a daily basis."

ANDRES: "Did you know him before that as well, when you were younger?"

VITALE: "Yes, but I didn't spend much time with him."

ANDRES: "Who taught you to swim?"

VITALE: "He did."

ANDRES: "During the time period after you got your catering truck, who was your best friend?"

VITALE: "Joe Massino."

ANDRES: "Who was the best man at your wedding?"

VITALE: "Joe Massino."

ANDRES: "Throughout your association of twenty-five years with the Bonanno Family, have you reported to one person or more than one person?"

VITALE: "Just one person."

ANDRES: "Who was that?"

VITALE: "Joe Massino."

ANDRES: "During the course of your association with the Bonanno Family, did you ever hold a higher position than Joseph Massino?"

VITALE: "Never."

ANDRES: "Did there come a time when your relationship changed with Mr. Massino?"

VITALE: "Yes, it did."

ANDRES: "When was that?"

VITALE: "Mid-nineties."

ANDRES: "Can you explain how it changed?"

VITALE: "Well, ever since Joe Massino made me underboss, he put a wedge in that period of time between me and the captains, leaving me in a very vulnerable position. There was nothing I wouldn't have done for the man, but he took the captains away from me. They weren't allowed to call me, they weren't allowed to give me Christmas gifts. When I got indicted on my own in November '01, none of the captains called me. I didn't get no support from the men. I felt that my wife and kids were going to be left in the street. That's why I decided to do what I am doing today."

ANDRES: "You said that Mr. Massino took away the captains from you. What does that mean?"

VITALE: "In other words, I had the position as underboss, but the captains couldn't call me, associate with me, make me earn any money. I was more or less, using our terminology, shelved. You might have the title but you are not doing anything. You are just, for lack of a better word, a figurehead."

It was a vacation to remember. Bonanno captain Frank Coppa and Joe Massino took their wives on a lavish European getaway in the late nineties, to celebrate the big man's birthday in style. Coppa and Massino had been business associates for years, and in the years after Massino was released, the two men made millions together and became close friends. Though the traveling foursome didn't possess a shred of sophistication between them, they spent their dollars like European aristocrats. Sweeping their way from Paris to Monte Carlo, they stayed in five-star hotels, ate in alfresco restaurants and shopped until their feet ached. Wearing spotless white sneakers, sensible slacks and short-sleeve shirts, Coppa and Massino might have passed for overweight

Midwestern sightseers. Like the hordes of other Americans in Europe, the couples took happy snapshots of each other standing in front of grandiose buildings and statues. One photograph, which made them all laugh for years, was taken of the men standing at either end of a tiny red Fiat. The two portly gangsters looked like giants beside a windup toy. In Paris, Massino bought his dear old friend a gift of rosary beads. Coppa treasured them: he placed them carefully in his wallet and carried them everywhere for the rest of the trip (and years after). It was the least Massino could have done. After all, it was Coppa who paid the entire expense of the vacation.

Coppa was from Bensonhurt, Brooklyn. Like his longtime friend, Frank Lino, Coppa earned his criminal bona fides burglarizing houses and hanging out on Avenue U. Coppa finished high school and even spent a few months in college, but after a few legitimate jobs—in a grocery store, driving a truck and waiting tables—he learned that crime was much more profitable. Coppa made his first real dollars handling swag, once pocketing close to twenty thousand dollars from a load of stolen watches and furs. In rough-and-tumble Bensonhurst, he rubbed up against gangsters from the

Bonanno, Colombo and Genovese families. Eventually, it was the Bonannos he grew closest to.

Frank Coppa wasn't a killer; however, he was very much a Mafioso. Coppa was what is sometimes known in the mob as a "white-collar wiseguy." He wasn't a street guy, he was a businessman, and a very shady one at that. He used his position and connections to bend the rules; he cut corners, cheated on his taxes and ripped off the corporate system. Coppa was one of the mob's biggest players on Wall Street, and practically invented the pump and dump scheme, where he'd "box-in" a particular stock, artificially inflate the price and then dump his shares, leaving mom and pop investors with absolutely nothing. It was a trick he pulled for the better part of thirty years, making millions as he went. Coppa had parking garage leases, soda vending machine and coin-operated telephone contracts, and a chain of chicken rotisserie restaurants, which he once tried to float on the stock exchange. He even used his weight to win a city contract to bus handicapped children to and from school.

Like legitimate high-stakes stock trading, pumping and dumping could be a crapshoot, and in 1972 Coppa lost his fortune. To win it back, he invested heavily in a

Texas oil company called Tucker Drilling. When he had accrued a quarter of the stock to himself, he dumped it at four dollars a share, making hundreds of thousands of dollars. There was only one problem: he was busted. Coppa was sentenced to three years' "supervised release" and two years' unsupervised. Despite his conviction, he continued playing the stock market, using his gangster status to coerce brokerage houses into buying and selling what he wanted to buy and sell. Being a "stock fixer" worked fine until he got caught again, along with his old pal Frank Lino: in 1992, they were both convicted of fraud.

Frank Coppa was released from prison in the late nineties, and immediately went back to work. By then, Joe Massino was off parole, and the two indulged in some joint racketeering. Massino even gave Coppa a loan to help him get back on his feet. As the money poured in, the two men grew closer. They had dinner regularly at CasaBlanca, where Coppa would hand the boss fifteen hundred dollars a week in tribute, as well as five thousand dollars to pay off his loan under the table. He became one of Massino's best earners—in the years Massino collected the Family tribute, Coppa gave him envelopes stuffed with cash totaling hundreds of thousands of dollars. Massino was so thrilled with the arrangement, he started bringing Coppa home for family dinners, introducing him into the inner Family circle.

The bad life was nothing but good to Frank Coppa. He drove a dark blue Mercedes SUV and lived in a sprawling house in Manalapan, New Jersey. He was powerful. He was rich. And thanks to the bulging envelopes he personally handed Massino each month, he was the boss's new best friend.

Frank Coppa was a whale of a man: when he strapped a belt around his plus-sized pants, his belly bulged out both above and below his waistline. He was a gentle giant with a demeanor that was more friendly bus driver than wiseguy. He wasn't so nice after he turned on Massino—but he was still rich.

BREITBART: "During the period of time when you were being debriefed by the agents in this case, did you get asked by them what assets you have?"

COPPA: "Yes."

BREITBART: "Did you indicate to them that it's been your practice to hide your assets?"

COPPA: "Not when they asked about it."

BREITBART: "You told them something about how you had a box with cash in it, right?"

COPPA: "Yes."

BREITBART: "Did you tell them how much cash was in the box?"

COPPA: "Yes."

BREITBART: "How much?"

COPPA: "Between cash and gold, a couple of hundred thousand."

BREITBART: "Did you turn that over to the government?"

COPPA: "No."

BREITBART: "That is still under your control?"

COPPA: "Not under my control, but under my wife's control."

BREITBART: "Do you consider your wife loyal to you?"

COPPA: "Yes."

BREITBART: "Your wife has access to those hundreds of thousands of dollars?"

COPPA: "Yes."

BREITBART: "If you told her to bring you $1.87, she would bring it?"

COPPA: "Maybe $2."

BREITBART: "Maybe $2. If you told her to bring one thousand dollars, she would bring one thousand dollars."

COPPA: "Yes."

BREITBART: "So it would be fair to say that the money is under your control?"

COPPA: "Yes."

BREITBART: "And would it be fair to say that you are holding that couple of hundred thousand dollars at a point in time when you have been ordered by a federal district judge to give five million dollars in restitution; is that right?"

COPPA: "Yes."

BREITBART: "Do you believe you are going to keep your assets?"

COPPA: "Hopefully."

The men who sat at Massino's table in the CasaBlanca restaurant were part of a small and very exclusive club. They were senior figures in the Family whom Massino trusted with his private life and personal investments: the likes of Frank Coppa, Richie Cantarella and Anthony Graziano, who were both his closest business associates and his friends. But things were different than they had been in the seventies and eighties. Back then, Massino had been a captain (even when he was acting as boss). He had surrounded himself with street guys like him: professional car thieves, loan sharks and killers. Massino was a crime commander, and they were his troops.

But now, as the official boss of the Family in a new decade, Massino had no use for street guys. He needed earners. He was no longer interested in the gritty business of his older associates, or maintaining his loyalty to them—he wanted money, and lots of it. Coppa, Cantarella and Graziano got close to him because they could afford to; in return, they got access and special treatment. The earners could do no wrong as long as they kept giving the boss fat envelopes.

Every year, it seemed, Massino upped his own salary. At the time he got out of jail, he and Vitale split the two hundred dollars a month they got in tribute from every made guy. The figure jumped to seven hundred and fifty dollars and then fifteen hundred dollars, by which time Vitale had been cut out of the equation. By the late nineties, the Family's ranks had swelled to include more than a hundred goodfellas and close to a thousand associates. Tributes filtered up to Massino from every last one. The boss started to demand "Christmas gifts," like the dons of other Families had reputedly done. Richard Cantarella, perhaps Massino's top earner, was particularly generous during the holidays: he once gave his boss a twenty-five-thousand-dollar Christmas bonus. By the year 2000, Massino was raking in so much tribute money he could have retired.

They say money's the root of all evil—and maybe it's true. While Massino's release from prison marked the beginning of his Family's resurgence, it also was the root of his eventual downfall. He changed positions . . . and the position changed him. It would prove to be a tragedy of mythological proportions: Joey Massino would become a victim of his own greed.

SEVEN

PARKING COPS

Barry Weinberg set off from his New Jersey home for his café in Little Italy, the Dixie Rose Café, just as he did on most mornings. With rush hour traffic, it was perhaps an hour's drive. Weinberg, a chain-smoking businessman who also had money in parking garages, took his usual route that day in January 2001, cruising across the George Washington Bridge in his new plum-colored, ninety-thousand-dollar Mercedes. After spending a few minutes at the café, he took off again—it was Tuesday, the day he always went to one of his garages in Midtown Manhattan.

As Weinberg approached the garage, two officers in an NYPD patrol car pulled alongside him and motioned him to pull over. It was around 10 a.m., and the avenue was choked with traffic and pedestrians. Weinberg had broken no law he could think of, so he wound down his window to ask what the problem was. The police quietly informed him there were people who needed to talk to him and asked him to step out of the vehicle. They escorted him to a van parked behind their car and told him to get in the back. Two FBI agents, Jeffrey Sallet and Kim McCaffrey, and an agent from the Internal Revenue Service, were hunched inside.

Weinberg, who suffered from chronic nervous tension, shook even harder as they dropped their bombshell: the FBI had been watching him for a year. Agents Sallet and McCaffrey continued to say that they knew everything about his web of shady business dealings. They listed his crimes and his associates, some of whom were Mafiosi. They charged him with tax evasion and said there could be much more serious charges to come. He could go to prison, they threatened, for a long time. "Your life has changed," the agents explained, "but we are going to give you a choice." They would either take him immediately to a federal courthouse, where he would make his first appearance in front of a judge, or he could assist them with their investigation of the Bonanno Crime Family in return for leniency. They gave him fifteen minutes to decide.

Weinberg's mind was racing. Give up everything in an instant, he agonized, or take my chances with the Family hit men? It only took him about ten seconds to decide. "What do you want me to do?" he replied. With those words, Barry Weinberg became an informant. The FBI now owned him—if he changed his mind, he'd go to jail. And just so there'd be no second thoughts, the Feds forced him to sign an agreement that day. Within a few hours he was fitted with a microphone and transmitter, and put back on the street, Mulberry Street. That day he began work for the United States government, a job he would do almost every day for the next year.

When Jack Stubing was promoted to supervisory special agent of the FBI's Bonanno Squad, he got the narrow, windowless office at the far end of the twenty-second floor in the FBI's New York City office tower, located at 26 Federal Plaza, in lower Manhattan. Stubing's office was oddly shaped and austere, because the space was originally designed as two small polygraph rooms, which had subsequently been joined together. Now, there wasn't much in there beyond a couple of wooden bookcases. One was behind the desk and another on a side wall—both were built with hidden recesses behind them that allowed space for a metal bar that ran horizontally along the walls. The bars were left over from the room's interrogation days, when prisoners were handcuffed in place and left unattended. They were so firmly mounted, it was cheaper for the FBI to custom-build the bookcases than remove the bars.

As the head of the Bonanno Squad, Stubing was one of five organized crime supervisors on the floor. The others led the Colombo, Genovese and Russian squads, and an assistant special agent in charge, or ASAC (pronounced a-sac), was chief of the entire New York organized crime program. (The Gambino and Lucchese squads were housed in a satellite office in Kew Gardens, Queens.) The open-space office was brutally functional: each supervisor had an office that looked out onto a vast squad area, where desks were crammed into tight cubicles. The floor was covered by old, ratty carpet, made uglier by the fluorescent light streaming down from the ceiling. Everywhere, empty coffee cups competed for space with snapshots of children and dog-eared files, stuffed with surveillance folders and internal reports. It seemed like a modest environment for such a heavy task: stopping organized crime.

Stubing's office had been home to many a chief Bonanno sleuth, but he added his own touches to his new surroundings. He hung a framed poster from the film *Goodfellas* on the wall (he says it's the closest to the real thing) and put up a picture of the Brooklyn Bridge, his favorite jogging route. Stubing liked to turn the overhead lights off when he worked so he could think more clearly, leaving only his desk lamp for illumination. There, accompanied by the sounds of Sergei Prokofiev and other classical composers, he'd ponder his assault on the Bonanno Family. The squad members would shake their heads and joke that, in the light of the desk lamp, their leader looked like a Mafia don sitting under interrogation spotlight, but all Stubing could think about was nailing, or in this case chaining, Massino to the wall.

Jack Stubing was one of the last O.C. agents from the glorious eighties, when the FBI first used RICO to wreak havoc upon the mob. It was up to him to pass on that decade of institutional knowledge—with a new batch of handpicked recruits before him, Stubing set to work schooling the eager newcomers with what his bosses had taught him. "I tried to pour everything in my head into their heads," he told me. He drilled them on old-fashioned investigative techniques and stressed that the battles against Italian organized crime from the seventies and eighties were still ongoing. Many of the cold case homicides from past mob wars had never been solved, and the men suspected of committing them—like Massino—were still on the street and more powerful than ever. Stubing brought retired FBI heroes into the office to give his recruits pep talks. Frank Spero and Matty Tricorico, the agents that flipped Sammy "The Bull" Gravano, stopped by, as did Joseph Pistone (Donnie Brasco), who at the time was in New York working on his TV show *Falcone*. "These were people they'd seen on TV and read about in books," said Stubing. "I wanted them to meet the living museum pieces, and have explained how it gets done."

Stubing had wanted to nail Massino ever since they'd first met. It was outside King Catering in 1993, not long after the new mob boss got out of jail—Stubing just wanted to let Massino know the Bureau was still interested. He found the big man hovering over the stove when he arrived at the door. He started slow, dangling pieces of inside information, hoping that Massino would take a nibble (the idea being to bounce Mafia innuendo off his opponent and study his reactions). Stubing often pretended to know more than he actually did. The trick could sometimes solicit a confirming gesture or sniffing denial.

Massino, however, was a veteran of such encounters, and had seen many an ambitious young agent come and go during his career. He batted away the newcomer with mocking charm—he even joked he knew the FBI had been watching him, and taunted the agent with tidbits about the nosy G-men who'd been slinking around since he'd gotten home. Stubing was shocked when Massino recited just about every make and model of vehicles in the FBI's surveillance fleet. He knew the cars' license plate numbers and described the agents who drove them, complete with sizes, hair and eye color.

Throughout the conversation, Massino gave Stubing the old honest businessman routine, saying he did nothing nowadays but cook, but the glint in Massino's eyes told a different story. The comedy sketch went back and forth until the frustrated agent finally came clean. "I haven't been able to catch you doing anything, so I'll have to assume you're not, unless I'm just stupid." Having won the joust, Massino looked Stubing dead in the eyes and gave his first straight answer, "You're not stupid."

"It was eye-opening, astonishing. This was a guy who had his wits about him," recalled Stubing in an interview. "I knew from that conversation, and it always stuck with me, that anything in our traditional toolbox wasn't going to work against him. He knew how we operated. He took very great precautions. He was very well disciplined and promoted people who were equally disciplined."

But by the time Stubing had taken over as supervisor, he had started to think outside the box, and it wouldn't be long before the tide would turn to his favor. During the investigation of Vitale's club, he'd subpoenaed boxloads of financial documents from the defendants—and suddenly was struck by an idea. Al Capone was nailed for income tax evasion. Could he do something similar with Massino? "They can kill witnesses, they can avoid talking on the phone, they can insulate themselves from potential informants," Stubing told me, "but what is this all about? Money. The money comes in, the money goes out. At some point it has to go through a legitimate financial institution so they can use it. And you can't kill a bank record."

As the Bonanno Family's power continued to grow, Stubing gently urged his superiors to begin a financial investigation of Joe Massino. He knew how hard it would be to change the culture of the FBI, but he was convinced that going over Massino's business records with a fine-toothed comb was the only way to build a RICO case against him. But to follow the money, Stubing knew he would need help. The FBI's O.C. accountants only had rudimentary bookkeeping skills, which were mostly used to keep track of expenses and money being paid to informants. Nobody on the squad knew how to identify a rubber check, let alone fuzzy accounting from a huge business.

In a series of conversations with his ASAC, Kevin Donovan, Stubing pleaded for more help. "If I could get an accountant in here," he said, "someone who knows what they are looking at, I could get Joe Massino." "Listen," replied Donovan. "Accountants automatically go to the white-collar branch. They need them to study bank fraud and the like. Your chances of getting one in here are between slim and none." Stubing was unmoved. He understood the problem and knew just what he needed to solve it: an expert accountant who didn't just tally figures but could actually drill down into shady financial information.

He didn't realize it at the time, but Stubing had unwittingly stumbled into a relatively new field of "forensic accounting," which incorporates accounting techniques into legal investigation. In the late nineties, big accounting firms like KPMG and Arthur Andersen were just discovering the power of forensic accounting. (Today, they employ huge teams dedicated to the field.) At the time, however, the FBI had never used forensic accounting as an investigative technique against the mob. Stubing's case against Massino's enterprise would be the first of its kind.

Special Agent Kimberly McCaffrey displayed perfect posture as she sat in the witness box at Massino's trial in 2004. The former champion gymnast perched herself on the seat with her chin up and shoulders back. Wearing a sensible dark suit, she spoke with the clipped sentences of an authority figure. The thirty-two-year-old special agent had good reason to sit up straight: she and her FBI partner, Jeff Sallet, sitting at the prosecution table in front, had been quietly building a case against Joseph Massino for five years, and that day they finally got to present it to a jury.

ANDRES: "You testified that you were conducting a financial investigation; can you explain to the jury what a financial investigation is?"

McCAFFREY: "We look into sources of income and expenses, and at the hierarchy of the Family, looking for financial associations, financial crimes."

ANDRES: "When you say hierarchy of the Family, what does that mean?"

McCAFFREY: "Joe Massino and Salvatore Vitale."

ANDRES: "You said you were looking into financial associations; can you explain what you understood a financial association to be?"

McCAFFREY: "A financial association is being owners in a business, properties, things of that nature."

ANDRES: "You said you were involved in a financial investigation; can you explain to the jury what investigative techniques you used?"

McCAFFREY: "We used grand jury subpoenas, interviews,

surveillances, reviewing of bank documents, financial records."

ANDRES: "Did you determine from those documents that there were certain financial associations?"

McCAFFREY: "Yes, we did."

Kim McCaffrey and her partner, Jeff Sallet, were both certified practicing accountants, as well as FBI agents. And the two were single-mindedly dogged in their pursuit of Massino. Having both been raised on a diet of American pie, they shared the belief that they'd signed on with the FBI to do right.

McCaffrey had been a talented gymnast in her youth. From age five to twenty-one, she trained five days a week and was so talented she made the junior Olympic team. During her senior year in high school, she fell eight feet from the uneven bars and landed in a handstand position, popping her elbows out of their sockets. The joints are still slightly crooked from the fall. "I was a nerd. I didn't drink in high school. I didn't go out. I didn't have time to get into trouble." In college, McCaffrey studied sports management and physical education, but she soon realized she'd have a better shot of getting a job if she wore a suit to work, so she decided to give accounting a shot. It turned out she was as good with a spreadsheet as she was on the uneven bars. The first seed of interest in government work was planted in a CPA class: a recruiter from the FBI came to give a talk and said the bureau needed accountants. McCaffrey was intrigued and took the woman's card. She applied and landed a spot at the Bureau's training academy in Quantico, Virginia.

While McCaffrey was tumbling through her Jersey childhood, Jeff Sallet was in New England rooting for the Red Sox. But Sallet never dreamed of playing in the major leagues—he was more brain than brawn. An exceptional student, Sallet got straight A's in high school without ever breaking a sweat. During his college years, he was social chairman at his fraternity as well as being in charge of rush. ("Rush is like recruiting cooperating witnesses," he would later joke.) After graduating, Sallet went to work at Ernst & Young and then Arthur Andersen, and then on to the New York FBI in the late nineties. Besides being far too close to a sea of Yankees fans, Sallet felt right at home—he found a new love playing real-life cops and robbers. He bounded into the office each day, read every mob book he could get his hands on and religiously followed the newspaper coverage of the cases he was involved with. But Sallet was dead serious when it came to hunting down Joey Massino. It was, after all, a potentially dangerous game.

Before joining the Bonanno Squad, both McCaffrey and Sallet cut their teeth on an "applicant" squad, where they did background checks with other new recruits. Sallet told his applicant squad supervisor he wanted to use his accounting skills to combat organized crime. The supervisor happened to be friends with Jack Stubing, who he knew was looking for accountants. Stubing, who by then was desperate to begin a financial investigation of Massino, immediately nabbed the young talent before any other team could get hold of him. In the meantime, McCaffrey had joined the New York office and done her time on an applicant squad and then a surveillance team. Having grown up in New Jersey, a hotbed of organized crime, she too wanted to use her accounting background to fight the Mafia. She joined the Bonanno Squad and was partnered with Jeff Sallet.

Stubing could hardly believe his luck. In three months, he went from having no accountants to having two. In early 1999, Stubing gave his two new agents a thin folder of background information and told them to go to it. At the time, McCaffrey was just twenty-six and Sallet was one year her senior.

On a cold day in February 1982, Bonanno associate Richard "Shallackhead" Cantarella helped kill his own cousin. Cantarella lured Anthony Mirra to a parking garage on North Moore Street in Lower Manhattan. As Cantarella and his uncle Al "Al Walker" Embarrato kept watch outside, another cousin, Joey D'Amico, climbed into Mirra's silver Volvo and shot him at point-blank range. When the NYPD tapped on the window hours later, Mirra looked like he was sleeping: his head had fallen forward so that his chin rested on his chest, and his eyes were closed. But blood coming from his ears indicated otherwise. Three bullets had struck him in the right side of the head, two behind the ear and one in the cheek. A forth bullet had lodged in his left knee. So much blood had drained down inside Mirra's jacket and into the seat of his pants that even his yellow under-wear was saturated with red.

Cantarella had been ordered to kill Mirra, a Bonanno soldier, by Joey Massino. The hit was payback for the Donnie Brasco infiltration. Mirra was another gangster who'd been taken in by the smooth-talking undercover agent, Joe Pistone. After Massino had Sonny Black murdered the year before, Mirra went into hiding, fearful he was next—and he was right. Massino figured his target would trust his own family, so he dispatched Mirra's cousins on the hit. He knew Richie Cantarella was prepared to do whatever it took to get ahead in the mob. Murder, even of a cousin, was strictly business, and Cantarella put in many a ruthless day on the job on his way to the senior ranks of the Bonanno Crime Family.

Cantarella was a skinny kid with jet-black hair who grew up in the bustling corridors of Knickerbocker Village, a housing development on the Lower East Side of Manhattan that sat directly behind the old *New York Post* building. Built at the end of the Depression for middle-income families, the village was the first major public housing project in the city. Cantarella went to work for the *Post* in the sixties, driving a delivery truck. He had an inside connection: his uncle Al Walker was one of the aging, old-school mobsters who had masterminded the Family's infiltration of the *Post* distribution center. Both his nephews, Cantarella and D'Amico, were his muscle in the loading docks.

But soon, Cantarella grew tired of being ordered around by his uncle and driving trucks. He got to know a corrupt city official named Rick Mazzeo, who gave out commercial leases at the city's ferry wharfs. Cantarella tattletaled on a newspaper stand tenant at the Lower Manhattan ferry terminal who was taking illegal sports bets; Mazzeo evicted the tenant and let Cantarella take over the stand. Every month, he gave Mazzeo kickbacks, and in return, Mazzeo threw more and more leases his way. With each new lease, the kickbacks got bigger.

Cantarella hit a small snag when he was arrested in the late seventies after writing a bad check for seven thousand dollars to a man who supplied cigarettes and candy to his newsstands. But by that time, his reputation preceded him: when Cantarella turned up at the courthouse to face the charges, the supplier approached him outside. He'd done his homework, he said, and he knew who Cantarella was. "I don't want no problems," the man whispered. "I'm dropping the charges." "I don't know what you're talking about," Cantarella replied. "Do what you want." The man never showed up for the court proceeding, and Cantarella walked.

By the late eighties, the wiseguy and the ferry guy had newspaper stands on both the Staten Island and Manhattan sides of the New York Harbor. They were making a fortune; despite officially being on a fifteen-thousand-dollar salary, Mazzeo drove a Mercedes with the vanity plate "Gatzby." The two men became so close, they shared an apartment in upper Manhattan. Over the years, they made hundreds of thousands of dollars out of their lease scams. But eventually, the high life got to be too much for Gatzby. He developed a drug habit and got fired from his city job. Cantarella didn't spare his pal any sympathy.

Shallackhead Cantarella had turned gray by the time he testified against Massino in 2004. His trademark slicked-down jet-black hair, which gave him his nickname, had gone the way of his vow of silence: it no longer existed. But when Assistant U.S. Attorney Mitra Hormozi questioned him, he detailed his crimes with the same business-as-usual approach he took to being a criminal.

HORMOZI: "Who was involved in Rick Mazzeo's murder?"

CANTARELLA: "Me, my uncle Al, my cousin Joey D'Amico and a fellow called Patty Muscles."

HORMOZI: "Describe the setup. How did you all kill Mr. Mazzeo?"

CANTARELLA: "There was a garage in, I think, Maspeth, Queens, on the borderline of Queens or Brooklyn, I'm not sure, on Varick Street. The place was owned by a fellow by the name of Mike DiBenedetto. Rick, he went there to look for a job; he was asking Mike for a job. He was out of work, Rick Mazzeo. We became aware of it and at that point we set up killing him. We met that night at Patty Muscle's—"

BREITBART: "Objection to the 'we,' judge."

JUDGE GARAUFIS: "All right, we have to specify, sir."

CANTARELLA: "I'm sorry."

HORMOZI: "When you say 'we' who are you referring to?"

CANTARELLA: "Me and Joey D'Amico met at Patty Muscle's auto shop. Patty Muscles and another individual. At the time, they were cleaning and loading the guns."

HORMOZI: "How many guns, do you recall?"

CANTARELLA: "Well, I got one. I believe there was three."

HORMOZI: "Okay."

CANTARELLA: "From there, me, Joey D'Amico and Patty Muscles went to this garage, it was an industrial garage someplace where trucks back in to load up, I don't remember what kind of stuff it was, and we proceeded to wait for Rick Mazzeo to come."

HORMOZI: "And once Rick Mazzeo arrived, what happened?"

CANTARELLA: "I met with Rick Mazzeo in Mike DiBenedetto's office, and they were talking; then I walked Rick Mazzeo out of his office to the garage area, I asked him what kind of car he was driving. Rick was always into cars and he went out and got his car, brought it into the garage. I said, let's go look at the car and while he was walking down the steps, I shot him in the back of the head."

HORMOZI: "Did anyone else shoot?"

CANTARELLA: "Another shot was fired I believe from Joey D'Amico."

HORMOZI: "What happened after he was shot?"

CANTARELLA: "After he was shot, he was laying on the floor bleeding, and he was dead. We picked him up,

Patty Muscles and Joey. Patty is a very big guy, that's why he'd got the nickname Patty Muscles, and we put him in a black plastic garbage bag and put him in the trunk of the car, and my cousin Joey then walked over and stabbed him in the back. With that we closed the trunk, I wiped off the entire car with a damp cloth. Patty and Joey took the car with the body in the trunk and went someplace with it, and I stayed behind with Mike Benedetto to clean the place."

HORMOZI: "Mr. Cantarella, did you get permission from anyone to kill Rick Mazzeo?"

CANTARELLA: "I got it from my uncle Al."

With powerful friends in Little Italy, Cantarella continued to make a killing. He bought a house in an upmarket neighborhood on Staten Island and began building an empire of parking lots. He also got to know Joe Massino—the two had met at the Toyland social club on Hester Street (which was operated by Rastelli's consiglierie Steve "Stevie Beef" Cannone) in the seventies. After a brief stint in jail in the mid-nineties following the bust at the *Post,* Cantarella got out at roughly the same time as when Massino came off parole. With money to spread around, Cantarella was quickly brought into Massino's inner circle, and the men ate dinner together every week at CasaBlanca. The boss liked Richie's style, and his bank balance even more. Cantarella's son was inducted into the Family in 1996, and three years later, Cantarella became a captain and was given his own crew.

Organized crime investigators like McCaffrey and Sallet take the opposite approach to the average detective. Under normal circumstances, when a crime is committed, the police investigate—they go to the crime scene, collect evidence and speak to witnesses. Then they try to deduce what happened and who is responsible. Not so for Mafia investigators. When the Mafia murders, it does so in private. Nobody calls the cops, there is rarely a body and there usually aren't any witnesses. Before a Mafia investigator begins, he or she must first identify the organization, pinpoint the players, figure out who their associates are and identify what rackets they are engaged in. Only at that point can they actually try to catch a suspect in the act of committing a crime.

In the late nineties, the FBI knew few details about the state of the Bonanno Family and the reemergence of Massino. His ability to stay off the radar screen had, in some ways, lulled the Bureau to sleep. In fact, when Sallet and McCaffrey started their probe, there was only a scant knowledge of the inner workings of the Bonanno crew. The agents were given a thin dossier of background information and were told the names of the suspected Bonanno captains. They assumed the Family was engaged in classic mob rackets like gambling and loansharking, but had no idea which captains were running which business, where it was being done or who the customers were. To top it all off, the number-one aide to mob investigators—informants—were virtually nonexistent when it came to the Bonannos.

Their supervisor believed the only way to dismantle the Bonanno Family was to start from the top. Stubing felt sure that if he could cut off the head, the body would die. He instructed McCaffrey and Sallet to target the boss himself and not to bother with petty cases against underlings. And that's just what they did.

The young agents' first task was to build a profile of Joseph Massino's assets. They knew he owned a house in Howard Beach and the CasaBlanca restaurant. But what else? There was no way the name "Joseph Massino" would pop up on a records search. A disciplined mobster never put holdings or businesses in his own name—he used front companies and nominees. McCaffrey and Sallet asked themselves who Massino's likely nominees might be: Josephine, his wife, and his three daughters were obvious choices. Thus the agents began the marathon process of data mining financial and legal institutions looking for leads. Every time they got a whiff of something, they'd go to the sitting grand jury on organized crime, get a subpoena and dig a little deeper. One avenue of inquiry led to Massino's accountancy firm, Garyn & Garyn. Massino instructed his lawyer, Sheldon Eisenberger, to try to quash the subpoena. His speedy reaction intrigued the agents, and government prosecutors renewed the fight to convince the grand jury that any documents involving Massino or his associates should be handed over by the firm. In the end, the decision came down in favor of the government.

On a hot June day in 1999, McCaffrey and Sallet arrived at Sheldon Eisenberger's office, located on Broad

Street in Manhattan's Financial District. Because of the fight over the documents, Eisenberger had hold of them for safekeeping. The lawyer's secretary handed the agents four medium-sized boxes. Dressed in street clothes for the task, McCaffrey and Sallet hauled the boxes down to Broad Street, laughing all the way because the boxes had *Playboy* written on the sides, and started the twenty-minute walk back uptown to the FBI's officer tower. By the time they got back, they were dripping with sweat—but the real work had just begun.

The partners rode the cool elevators up to the twenty-second floor and flopped down at their desks. As they began spreading the boxes' contents out, they found what they'd expected from an accounting firm: income tax returns, receipts and returned checks. Most of it was administrative junk. But three little checks they found kicking around in the vast piles of paper didn't smell quite right. They'd been written by Dianna Vitale—Sal Vitale's wife—to a name the agents didn't recognize: Barry Weinberg. One was for ten thousand dollars. Written on the memo line was "Lexus 24." Another was for $16,666.50, with a note saying "Stonehurst," and another, for five thousand dollars, had "Stable" on the memo line. The agents knew they had a lot of work to do to decipher the mysterious checks, but one question immediately stood out: who was Barry Weinberg?

Barry Weinberg and Cantarella had been close business associates for twenty years. Weinberg, a shrewd Jewish businessman who grew up in Sheepshead Bay, Brooklyn, had followed his father into the parking lot business. He and Cantarella met when Cantarella answered Weinberg's ad in the *New York Times* for a parking garage lease. The men became partners in Stable Parking, a run-down Little Italy lot where cars were hoisted to upper levels in an elevator.

Weinberg was a fixture on Mulberry Street. He was a nervous little character who walked with hunched shoulders and a cigarette permanently pressed between his lips. He was also a ladies' man who had children with three different women. But he was generous to all his children and worked hard to put them through school. Each day, he drove to the Dixie Rose Café— jointly owned by him and Cantarella under a nominee's name—on the corner of Broome and Mulberry. (It has since become part of Umberto's Clam House, the site of Crazy Joe Gallo's assassination in 1972.) There, he and Cantarella would pal around with the neighborhood wiseguys, drink coffee and nibble on Italian pastries. After the Dixie Rose was sold, the group moved their meeting spot across the street to the famous Caffe Roma, and later to Da Nico's Ristorante a couple of doors down. Even though he wasn't Italian, the Family men liked Weinberg. The wisecracking Jew was good company, and more important, he was rich.

Weinberg spent his working weeks rubbing elbows with high-ranking Bonannos, but he never became part of the family. He was what's known in mob-speak as an associate: he did business with the Mafia and enjoyed the privileges his criminal buddies afforded him, but he wasn't a made member. He had the backing of mob heavies when it came to securing a lease or winning a contract, and in return his gangster friends got a taste of his business. But Cantarella enjoyed being nasty and made a great sport of belittling Weinberg. He never left any doubt in Weinberg's mind as to who was in charge. The mobster would tease Weinberg's hardnosed business style by saying, "Always the Jews, always the Jews." Weinberg didn't mind the taunts as long as the money kept coming, but he knew he was in a precarious position. He was often finding himself on the bad end of business deals. Even when he did okay, there was no hiding the fact that Cantarella was using him.

As the years went by, Cantarella's appetite for Weinberg's money increased—once he became a captain, he began demanding bigger and bigger slices of the profits. By the late nineties, Cantarella had dropped all pretense of a partnership and was flat-out extorting his old friend. He demanded a piece of everything Weinberg was into, and beginning in 1998, he frightened Weinberg into writing him a string of fat checks. One was for one hundred thousand dollars; another was for sixty thousand dollars and another, one hundred and twenty-five thousand dollars. To cover himself, Cantarella had legal papers drawn up saying Weinberg loaned him the money. In two years, all told, he forced Weinberg to hand over eight hundred thousand dollars.

Joe Massino and his associates found creative ways to protect their illegal earnings—after all, there was no point in stealing and extorting piles of cash if you couldn't spend it. That meant Massino laundering a portion of his money while at the same time showing a legitimate income. On his tax returns in the nineties, Massino claimed he'd won the lottery on two separate occasions. In reality, Massino used his street contacts to buy the winning tickets before they'd been cashed in. It worked out for everyone, because Massino paid the owner of the ticket more than the person would have been paid had they cashed in the ticket and then incurred the winning pot. Instead Massino handed in the ticket and got a lottery receipt, which he could show the Internal Revenue Service if he got audited. Of course, the lottery winnings were a mere pittance in the scope of what Massino was really making.

In 1992, while he was still on parole, Massino started eyeing Cantarella's parking lot empire. He had Vitale approach Cantarella to inform him he'd be selling part of the three businesses to Massino. There was no financial incentive for Cantarella, but he couldn't very well refuse the boss. However, Cantarella wasn't about to give up his piece of the action—he made Weinberg do it. Legal papers were drawn up, and Massino and Vitale bought out part of Weinberg's share of Cantarella's parking lot businesses at well below market price: for $10,000, $16,666.50, and $5,000, respectively. (Tax returns for the first garage, Lexus 24, located on East Twenty-fourth Street, Manhattan, showed its gross income rising from $182,000 in 1994 to $337,000 in 2001. At the second garage, Stonehurst Parking Corp., on Stone Street in Manhattan, the gross income grew from $300,121 in 1994 to $305,109 in 2001.)

Massino's purchase of Weinberg's share in the parking garages was as legitimate as his business deals got— he did actually pay Weinberg for the properties, albeit well below what he should have. But ironically, the parking garage deal would turn out to be the first concrete RICO evidence the FBI could gather against him. Seven prosperous years after he'd bought into the lots, the three checks his brother-in-law's wife had written for the businesses turned up in the *Playboy* boxes, which found their way to New York's Bureau headquarters. It didn't take McCaffrey and Sallett long to figure out that "Lexus," "Stonehurst" and "Stable" were parking garages connected to Weinberg and Cantarella. Now they had irrefutable proof that there was a business relationship between Weinberg and Massino.

The agents were beginning to piece the puzzle together. They swung their full attention to Weinberg, putting him under twenty-four-hour surveillance and conducting a full-blown forensic accounting investigation into his business empire. As new names and places poured in from the surveillance team over the next twelve months, McCaffrey and Sallet used spreadsheets to keep track of everything. (After all, they were accountants.) They keyed in every one of Weinberg's associates, every business he was involved in and, most importantly, the long list of financial and racketeering crimes he was committing. Sure, they could have nailed Weinberg for failing to pay his taxes, but he was potentially far more useful if they could keep him on the street. The agents' plan was to collect so much evidence against Weinberg that when it came time to confront him, they could easily convince him to become an informant. Weinberg was no hardened criminal, and the agents knew the thought of going to prison would terrify him. He had an adoring elderly mother and a large, dependent brood. It seemed unlikely Weinberg would give up his liberty for the sake of a couple of degenerate mobsters.

The day of the dramatic Midtown Manhattan arrest, McCaffrey and Sallet got to test their theory. Having identified Weinberg's pattern, they knew that every Tuesday morning he went to a certain garage in

Midtown. The FBI chose to make the arrest there because they knew Weinberg didn't have any Mafia pals who operated in the area—it was unlikely any wiseguys would notice him being hauled into a van. That morning, they watched as Weinberg left his New Jersey home and made his way toward New York City. They followed with the van, and at a prearranged point, NYPD officers joined the procession. Before he reached the garage, the officers swooped.

After he agreed to cooperate, Sallet and McCaffrey whisked Weinberg down to Federal Plaza. He was led into an interview room and presented with a cooperation agreement and a pen. He signed in front of an assistant U.S. attorney and was quickly debriefed about his crimes. The agents had to move fast so that Weinberg wouldn't be missed—they put a recording device on him right then and there, and by the afternoon he was making tapes. Just like that, Weinberg was in for good. There was no way he could go back on his agreement without going immediately to jail.

The bright red awning of Da Nico's Ristorante is a landmark in Little Italy. The famous Italian eatery, located at

164 Mulberry Street, is in the heart of the downtown neighborhood. The sprawling restaurant has a large outdoor dining area, which is packed almost every summer night with politicians, actors and tourists alike.

In 2004, *New York Post* reporter Kati Cornell Smith dropped a bombshell when she revealed allegations that the owner of Da Nico's, Perry Criscitelli, was a made member of the Bonanno Family. At the time, Criscitelli was a pillar of Little Italy's community: he had interests in four local restaurants and was president of the San Gennaro feast, the neighborhood's number-one annual street fair. His wife was the event's treasure. Up until the mid-nineties, the mob, and in particular the Genovese Family, famously controlled the feast, demanding extortionate amounts from stall holders. It was Rudy Giuliani—a frequent Da Nico's customer himself—who finally clamped down on the feast in 1996, installing an independent monitor to keep the mob out. During the summer months, Cantarella and his buddies would sit at the same table right outside the front door every night. Among them was Barry Weinberg—with the FBI listening through a microphone.

Weinberg was the perfect plant. He was a nervous character to begin with, so the men had no clue he was taping them. He just sat around as always talking about business, cars and women—just good old Barry. No one knew that he was secretly meeting McCaffrey and Sallet on nearby Howard Street Monday through Thursday afternoons, where the agents would secure a microphone and transmitter underneath his clothes before switching it on and making sure their receiving equipment was picking up the signal. Before he'd leave to go about his normal business, the agents made a short preamble on the tape stating their names, the time and date, and that they were giving the device to the cooperating witness. For the next five hours, the FBI heard every sound Weinberg or anyone around him made (even the sounds they didn't want to hear). At the end of the day, Weinberg would return to Howard Street and the agents would switch the device off. The cycle would start again the next morning.

They were long days for McCaffrey and Sallet, who had to listen to the tapes and transcribe any important information. McCaffrey would spend her morning and evening commutes listening to hours of mobsters giving away little more than sports reports and reviews of the latest Hollywood release. But it wasn't all tedium—often, she'd pick up a nugget of important information. Slowly but surely, the FBI quietly chased down leads and issued subpoenas. When he wasn't working the street, Weinberg was filling in the gaps in regular grilling sessions with agents and prosecutors, spilling every morsel of information he knew about Cantarella and Massino. As the days blurred together, a curious, although not unexpected, bond formed between the pugnacious little man, whose humor only partly concealed his sadness and fear, and the agents. In the end, Weinberg made eighty devastating tapes.

Made men are accustomed to having the FBI snoop around. Avoiding telephoto lenses and shaking off tails are just part of the job. But in late 2001, Cantarella had a bad feeling. Subpoenas were raining on the Family, and the surveillance cars seemed to be everywhere. He knew the Feds had the parking garage tax returns, and he feared it was only a matter of time before they connected the dots between him and the Bonanno hierarchy. He knew they were coming, and they knew he knew. The standoff became so blatant that, by the time of the September 11 attacks, McCaffrey and Sallet were regularly spotted wandering past Da Nico's. More than once Cantarella looked up to see the grinning agents staring back at him.

At that point, the agents' plan shifted slightly. Having built a solid foundation of evidence, they were now trying to scare the Bonanno captain into thinking an arrest was imminent: if he were in a panic to cover his tracks, he'd be more likely to make a mistake. McCaffrey and Sallet often ate lunch on Mulberry Street, watching their targets squirm on the other side of the street. On one occasion, Sallet wandered into Da Nico's itself and asked for a table for one. Cantarella and his pals sat dumbfounded at their regular table only a few feet away from where the agent was standing. A restaurant employee, who knew exactly who Sallet was, politely told the agent that no tables were available. But at that point, the agent had already accomplished his purpose.

As the noose tightened, Cantarella began to suspect Weinberg, but he was too smart to threaten or hurt him. Killing an informant would bring the full weight of the government down on him. Instead, he made nice. "We're all under a lot of heat," he calmly told his old friend. "Why don't you stay home for a while." McCaffrey and Sallet thought it wasn't a bad suggestion. No sense in pushing things too far. Weinberg was pulled off the street in 2002 and placed in the Witness Protection Program, along with his family. (He died of cancer shortly thereafter.)

Massino's defense attorney, David Breitbart, wore a black belt and a pistol at his side outside the courtroom. But during his cross-examination, words were his weapon of choice.

BREITBART: "Mr. Cantarella, my name is David Breitbart. I represent Mr. Massino, and I am going to ask you some questions on cross-examination. Have you been told, sir, that you were going to be cross-examined?"

CANTARELLA: "Sure."

BREITBART: "Were you told that I was going to be cross-examining you?"

CANTARELLA: "They told me Joe's lawyer was going to cross-examine me."

BREITBART: "Did you get any practice for cross-examination?"

CANTARELLA: "Practice?"

BREITBART: "Yes, did they take you into a courtroom, sit you in the box and . . ."

CANTARELLA: "No."

BREITBART: "Did there come a time when you went someplace into a room and someone practiced cross-examining you?"

CANTARELLA: "Yes."

BREITBART: "And who was that?"

CANTARELLA: "It was Greg Andres and that gentleman there named Robert."

BREITBART: "Mr. Henoch?"

CANTARELLA: "If that's his name."

BREITBART: "These two people at the end of the table."

CANTARELLA: "Yeah."

BREITBART: "Did they indicate to you that they were showing you what cross-examination was about?"

CANTARELLA: "Yes."

BREITBART: "How long did the procedure take?"

CANTARELLA: "The one with Greg, hour and a half, two hours. The one with Robert, half hour, forty-five minutes."

BREITBART: "So, what you are telling us is that on at least two separate occasions, for several hours, you were cross-examined by the government to prepare you for cross-examination, is that right?"

CANTARELLA: "I believe so."

BREITBART: "And when did Mr. Andres do the practice cross on you?"

CANTARELLA: "One day last week."

BREITBART: "And when did Mr. Henoch do the practice examination on you?"

CANTARELLA: "Last night."

Early one morning in August 2002, Cantarella and his wife, Loretta, heard someone bang on the door of their magnificent Staten Island home. When they answered, fifteen law enforcement officials and a search warrant confronted them. Led by McCaffrey and Sallet, a group of FBI agents and New York State police officers had arrived to rip the house apart. The Cantarellas were none too thrilled, but tried to conceal their nerves with a cheerful resolve. As McCaffrey and Sallet chattered politely with the Bonanno captain and his wife, the agents and officers went to work. They split up into small teams and combed through every room in the sprawling house. Drawers were turned upside down, closets were emptied and boxes were gone through. They went up into the attic and down into the basement.

As it turned out, most of what they were looking for was sitting right on or in Cantarella's safe.

That morning, the FBI confiscated telephone books listing Cantarella's Mafia associates, a list of license plate numbers from surveillance cars that had been following him, incriminating photographs, as well as a list of tribute payments he was entitled to from his men. More importantly, McCaffrey and Sallet turned up boxes of financial documents, which they removed one by one and took to a warehouse. The documents, which included tax returns for the three parking garages, provided further proof that Cantarella had a direct business association with Massino.

Cantarella was finished. They knew it and so did he. The agents went back to their office and waited for Cantarella to call.

EIGHT

DIGGING UP THE PAST

Howard Beach, Queens, is one of those New York neighborhoods that's not always safe for outsiders. When a young black man wandered into the grid of streets beside John F. Kennedy International Airport in 2005, he had his skull cracked open with a baseball bat. His attacker, Nicholas "Fat Nick" Minucci, appeared on the reality TV show *Growing Up Gotti* alongside John Gotti's grandsons. After Minucci was charged with a hate crime and jailed, his friends printed T-shirts that said "Free Fat Nicky." The neighborhood is the picture of suburbia with white fences, trimmed lawns and driveways full of SUVs—but that doesn't change the fact that it's the Mafia's zip code.

The area was home to Sonny Red's son, Bruno Indelicato, as well as a son-in-law to the Lucchese boss. Howard Beach's favorite son was, of course, John Gotti, who lived in a modest two-story home on Eighty-sixth Street. Gotti thought of himself as a kind of de facto mayor of the neighborhood: every July 4, he would stage an elaborate and highly illegal fireworks display for the benefit of his neighbors. One of those neighbors was Joseph Massino, who lived in a gaudy, faux-Georgian mansion a few minutes' walk from Gotti, complete with white Corinthian columns across its broad, brick facade. A couple more doors down the street lived Massino's daughter, Joanne. She would often bring her children to their grandparents' house on summer days to swim in the backyard pool and be spoiled rotten by their "Poppy," as they called Joe. Like the Gotti boys, Massino wasn't always so kind when outsiders ventured onto his territory: legend has it that when Joanne's future husband was celebrating his bachelor party with a group of friends, the boys got a bit overexcited when the strippers arrived. The father of the bride didn't appreciate having his daughter disrespected, so he had the groom beaten senseless. (Joanne and her husband have since parted company.)

Joseph Massino was at home on January 9, 2003, the morning Agents McCaffrey and Sallet knocked on his front door. He was already dressed and ready to go in a black velour sweat suit, his hair neatly combed. "You must be Kimberly, and you must be Jeffrey," he told the agents. He remarked that he'd expected them the previous day, as he'd seen surveillance cars in the street. (The cars had, in fact, been there for several days to make sure Massino didn't make a run for it before McCaffrey and Sallet could arrest him.) The agents, who were sporting the trademark blue Windbreakers with "FBI" written in yellow across the backs, were accompanied by a state policeman and an IRS agent. They stayed only a few minutes inside the house before handcuffing Massino and leading him outside. Josephine sat perfectly still at the kitchen table, staring at her husband and saying nothing.

Massino was placed in the backseat of the FBI car; McCaffrey got in the front passenger seat. As Sallet steered the vehicle onto the Cross Bay Boulevard and headed north toward Lower Manhattan, McCaffrey swiveled around to face the prisoner. Without a hint of prejudgment in her tone, she asked for his "pedigree information": age, height and weight, which she wrote down on a marshal intake form. Massino was friendly and personable in his replies. He joked that the agents must have "wired Barry [Weinberg] up a lot," and remarked that certain associates of his had "gotten to work quick." He had a pretty good idea which of his old pals was the first one to rat him out.

After arriving at FBI headquarters, Massino was escorted up to the twenty-second floor, where Nora Conley, second in command on the FBI's Bonanno squad, greeted him. He recognized her from an encounter at CasaBlanca and remarked, in his oddly jovial way, that she was like the "underboss" of the team. He was then fingerprinted, photographed and briefly interviewed. Massino revealed that he'd heard McCaffrey was a talented investigator who'd been recruited straight out of college. "Wow," said McCaffrey. "You know a lot about me." Massino replied, "You do your homework, I do mine."

That afternoon, Joseph Massino was charged with the murder of Dominick "Sonny Black" Napolitano. At the time, he was not offered a plea bargain of any kind. "We wanted justice to be done," McCaffrey later told me. Massino was handed over to the U.S. Marshal Service and driven to the Brooklyn Federal Courthouse. The magistrate judge denied him bail, and Massino was confined to a solitary cell in the nearby Metropolitan Detention Center to await trial. It was exactly two years to the day since McCaffrey and Sallet had arrested Barry Weinberg, and a day before Joseph Massino turned sixty.

At the secret initiation ceremony for new Bonannos, Massino always made the same speech. He told the recruits they were joining a family that had never known a rat. Not one made member of the clan had ever testified in court against his own—in the fifties, Bonannos had even gone to the electric chair rather than break their vow of silence. As the modern era's Last Godfather, Massino was proud of this legacy of silence, which harkened back to the Mafia's glory days in the early twentieth century; the fact that not one Bonanno had ever sung was a testament to the proud tradition. Perhaps it was because the Bonannos still had first-generation Sicilian blood in the family. Or maybe it was that the men were more frightened of Massino than they were of the government. For whatever reason, Joseph Massino inspired incredible loyalty from his men.

Everything changed in October 2002, when the FBI nailed ten Bonannos, including Family captain Frank Coppa. At the time, Coppa had just started a thirty-six-month prison sentence at Fort Dix, New Jersey, for securities fraud. The Feds now had him for, among other things, joining in the extortion of Barry Weinberg. Coppa suddenly found himself facing up to eighty more months in prison. The soft-spoken gangster called his lawyer and said he just couldn't do it. If the FBI would offer him a deal, he was ready to talk. At sixty-one years old, there was no way he was going to take his chances at another trial. All he wanted, he said, was to go back to his family.

Less than two weeks after Coppa was arrested, he became the first made Bonanno in history to turn on the Family. With one signature, he sold out Joey Massino and his hundred-year-old tradition, agreeing to detail every crime he'd ever committed in his forty-year career as a gangster, as well everything about the criminal activities of every other gangster he'd ever known. If the government was completely satisfied, Coppa's wife and one of his sons would be relocated from their home for their own protection. There was even a slim chance he would be let off the extortion charge and get off scot-free. After signing the deal, Coppa was transferred to a secure location, where he was grilled for ten straight days. In the end, the FBI had what it needed: enough evidence to arrest Massino.

On the same day Frank Coppa was arrested, a team of agents descended on the home of Richard Cantarella and took him, his wife, Loretta, and their son Paul into custody. Cantarella was charged with fifteen counts of racketeering, conspiracy to murder (Robert Perrino, the missing *New York Post* delivery superintendent), extortion, money laundering, arson, illegal bookmaking, loan-sharking and kidnapping. Up until then, the only prison time Cantarella had done was less than a year for his *New York Post* shenanigans—but had struggled through every hour of it. Now he was facing life in prison and, thanks to the Weinberg tapes, he knew he didn't stand a chance.

In January 2003, Cantarella pleaded guilty to two murders and agreed to testify for the government. He was removed from Brooklyn's Metropolitan Center and placed in protective custody; his wife and son, who were out on bail, quietly moved out of their home in Staten Island and disappeared into the Witness Protection Program.

After three years of painstaking detective work, the case against Joseph Massino was beginning to explode. Agents were pulled off other organized crime squads to help as the Bureau worked around the clock, extracting information and cross-checking stories. Because the cooperating witnesses (or "CW's," as the agents called them) were in great danger, the FBI hid them in hotel rooms across the city. Judge Nicholas Garaufis was shuttled around to the secret locations at odd hours of the day to sign off on cooperation agreements. He called himself the "stealth judge," and joked with the agents that he never wanted to be the first one to leave the room in case mob henchmen were laying in wait. The mood among top law enforcers was one of cautious excitement.

With Frank Coppa and Richie Cantarella's admissions behind them, the FBI had ample evidence to charge Massino with the murder of Sonny Black and a laundry list of racketeering crimes. But to get the charges to stick, they needed a corroborator. Only one man had been at Massino's side since the beginning. Only one man had been involved in practically every hit: Salvatore Vitale. If the FBI could get him to crack, Massino would spend the rest of his life locked inside a concrete box.

On the same day they picked up Massino, the FBI scooped up Vitale as well. He was arrested at his home in Long Island and charged, along with Cantarella, with the murder of Robert Perrino. Vitale was visibly nervous: he feared there was no escape. He could either sign on with the government or rot in prison. He knew that his cooperation with the Feds would turn the lives of his family upside down—his wife and sons would be forced to leave their jobs and friends and go into hiding. But whatever bridge of loyalty he had to his boss had long since been burned. Compared to the thought of life in prison without parole, ratting out Massino was the least of his concerns. Vitale signed his agreement in February, pleading guilty to eleven murders, and became the most senior mob member to turn since Sammy "The Bull" Gravano.

The FBI whisked Sal Vitale to an army base, where he was debriefed for two weeks solid. He showed them his "shy book" (where he kept track of his illegal loan-sharking transactions) and told them where they could find twenty thousand dollars in cash sealed under a tiled concrete floor. When it came time to talk about his relationship with Massino, Vitale took the prosecutors on a tour of Queens and Brooklyn, detailing the crimes of his brother-in-law with militarylike precision. He knew places, dates, times . . . everything. By the time it was over, the government had enough to get Massino on eight murders. Suddenly, a return to Howard Beach was looking like a very distant prospect for the Bonanno boss.

James "Big Louie" Tartaglione was an electrical worker by trade. At least, it said as much on his union card. As a member of Local 3 of the International Brotherhood of Electrical Workers, he wore a hardhat for four decades. The men at Local 3 strung power lines, dug holes for poles and laid cable. Big Louie was paid handsomely for his expertise, making up to $90,000 a year. But when he was busted in the mid-seventies, no amount of sweet-talking his union patrolmen brethren could get him off the hook. The truth was, Big Louie didn't know a watt from a volt. He made his real money after he laid down his tools at the end of the day and went to work as a loan shark.

According to testimony, Big Louie got his apprenticeship in loan-sharking at a social club in Brighton Beach, Brooklyn, owned by a man named Charlie Shoe. Shoe owed Big Louie a lot of money in the early seventies, so he made the shylock a partner in the illegal card game he ran out of the club, which paid a salary of one hundred dollars a week. Big Louie also got to lend money to the players, as well as his other marks. At any one time, he might have as many as fifteen loans out, some for tens of thousands of dollars. Loan sharks like Big Louie made their profits charging "extortionate" interest rates, or what they called points (one point is 1 percent a week). Depending on the amount of the loan, Big Louie charged between two points for, say, a ten-thousand-dollar loan, which brought in two hundred dollars a week, and five points on a one-thousand-dollar loan, which generated fifty dollars a week. He kept business flowing by targeting made and connected men he knew he could trust.

Through it all, Big Louie was a loyal soldier to Joe Massino. As a Bonanno associate, he relied on the Family's protection to give him muscle in the club and keep his operation safe from other gangsters who might have wanted a piece of the action. At one point, John Gotti—who, for a variety of reasons, believed Louie's tribute money should have gone to him—approached him at Charlie Shoe's and demanded restitution. "Louie," said Gotti, "you're with me, so the club belongs to me." Big Louie replied, "I'm not with you, John, I'm with Joe Massino." At the sit-down arranged to settle the dispute, Massino overpowered Gotti, settling the dispute once and for all: Big Louie would pay Joe Massino a cut of his business. Just the alliance with the Bonannos was enough to terrify any recalcitrant payer into coughing up the money they owed him.

For more than thirty years, Big Louie was one of Massino's closest aides. He was made on the same day as Vitale in 1983, and after just one year was promoted to captain. Under Massino's direction, Big Louie committed arson and carried out hits: he was one of Cesare's hit men, and once, on Vitale's orders, he disposed of the body of a man who robbed a Family captain of ten thousand dollars (even though he and Vitale never got along). When Massino got out of prison in 1993, Big Louie fell even further into the in crowd—he was put on the Family committee as treasurer and given the job of overseeing the war chest. As far as Joe Massino knew, Big Louie was one of the few people he could really trust.

But the truth was, after Louie was arrested for loansharking in 1997 (he pleaded guilty and got fifty-one months in Fort Dix, New Jersey), he was never the same. The prison time changed him. He'd been separated from his family and had gotten kicked out of Local 3, though he was still getting his pension. By the time he got out of prison in 2002, he wanted nothing more to do with committing "mortal sins," as he would later describe the Mafia's business. Despite Massino's pleas, Big Louie moved to Boca Raton, Florida, to begin again.

Massino's feelings were more hurt by Big Louie Tartaglione's betrayal than Sal Vitale's—it felt like his last true friend had abandoned him. And the evidence

Big Louie provided when questioned by U.S. Attorney
Mitra Hermozi did just as much damage to the Family.

HERMOZI: "What did you do after you learned that Sal
    Vitale had decided to cooperate with the govern-
    ment?"

TARTAGLIONE: "I wanted to cooperate with the govern-
    ment. I wanted to have the slate cleaned."

JUDGE GARAUFIS: "Could you just move back a little
    bit from the microphone?"

TARTAGLIONE: "I'm sorry."

JUDGE GARAUFIS: "It's the opposite of what we asked
    you to do before. You're a little close. Go ahead."

HERMOZI: "So Mr. Tartaglione, what did you do at
    that point?"

TARTAGLIONE: "I got ahold of my probation officer
    and I told him, I says, 'I'd like to get ahold of some-
    body,' which was Ruth Nordenbrook."

HERMOZI: "Why did you want to contact Ruth Nor-
    denbrook?"

TARTAGLIONE: "Because I felt I built a bond with her
    years ago. When she was first a prosecutor on my
    case she wasn't so nice, but we became friends. The

reason I felt a little bond is when my daughter got . . . she went to hospital. She was getting a mammogram, and she passed out while she was there, and I had called up my lawyer and my lawyer called up Ruth, and she says, 'By all means, let him go over there.' That's why I called her, because I knew she was warm."

HERMOZI: "Did you meet with Miss Nordenbrook?"

TARTAGLIONE: "Yes."

HERMOZI: "What were you asked during those meetings?"

TARTAGLIONE: "Actually, it's not what I was asked. I told them about myself and my criminal history and the things I knew about people."

HERMOZI: "So did the government eventually agree to sign a cooperation agreement with you?"

TARTAGLIONE: "Yes."

HERMOZI: "And as part of that cooperation agreement, did you agree to wear a recording device?"

TARTAGLIONE: "Yes."

HERMOZI: "Who did you wear a recording device against, generally?"

TARTAGLIONE: "Organized crime figures."

HERMOZI: "During your conversations with members of organized crime that you were recording, did you ask them about their participation in criminal activities?"

TARTAGLIONE: "No."

HERMOZI: "Why not?"

TARTAGLIONE: "Because once I asked them, they would turn around and say there's something going on here. And it's not—usually you don't ask a person what they did in their criminal activity, not unless they felt like volunteering and telling you."

HERMOZI: "Was Mr. Massino the subject of any of the conversations?"

TARTAGLIONE: "Oh, yes."

After Big Louie made his deal with the government, he returned to New York, saying he was back to help run the battered Family. In September 2003, he met with Anthony "Tony Green" Urso, who had been named acting boss after Vitale and Massino were arrested. The mood at the meeting was tense: Massino was in jail preparing for the trial of his life, and his men on the street were only too aware that a slew of their so-called *amici di amici* were working for the government. Tony Green was furious, especially with Vitale. Any day now, he fumed, they might be indicted too. Why should the children of "rats" be allowed to live, he ranted, when his kids would suffer if he went to prison? "It's gotta stop," he demanded, instructing Big Louie to talk to the men. "You tell them, 'Whoever turns, we'll wipe your family out.' If you take one kid—I hate to say it—and do what you gotta do, they'll fucking think twice. How would Sal feel if I killed one of his kids?"

What Tony Green didn't know was that at that moment, as he was talking tough about informants, one was standing right in front of him. An electronic device in the front pocket of Big Louie's jacket was transmitting every word out of Tony's mouth to an FBI tape recorder. Between May 2003 and January 2004, Big Louie made a total of forty-five tapes, suckering a bunch of senior Bonannos who were still fiercely loyal to their incarcerated boss into revealing information that would later be used to nail him to the wall. Big Louie was such a good informant, he made them believe that he too was one of the last true believers. "Joe trusts you," Tony Green said. "He knows that you're one hundred percent with him.

That's what it's all about. He has nobody anymore to trust. Who's he have? You, me . . . a few guys, that's all. And he told me he trusts you 'cause he knows you a long time. That's what it's all about, Lou, that's why he wants you here." Louie was able to look him in the eye and reply, "I got chills, hearing you say that."

As the FBI recorders rolled, it started to seem like no task was too dangerous for Big Louie. One time, the FBI sent him and a female undercover agent (playing the role of his girlfriend) to a nightclub in Long Island to try to tempt Tony Green with a load of supposedly stolen diamonds and gold. In an even more daring episode, he wore a wire to the office of a well-known criminal defense lawyer with an O.C. client base, who the FBI suspected had information about a three-thousand-dollar loan-shark payment. Four times Big Louie went to the office to try and get the lawyer to talk. He didn't bite, and eventually the line of inquiry was dropped, but it didn't make any difference. By the time Big Louie retired from his recording career, the Feds had a mountain of evidence on Massino. Combined with the information they'd extracted from Coppa, Cantarella and others, they had enough evidence to round up another bunch of Bonannos. In January 2004, just over a year after Massino was arrested, the FBI arrested eighteen more men, including Tony Green and the alleged acting underboss, Joseph Cammarono. The indictment included fifteen counts of murder. With that round of arrests, the FBI wiped out what remained of the Bonanno hierarchy. The Family, it seemed, was finished.

On July 30, 2004, Massino was found guilty on all eleven charges he faced, including seven counts of murder. (Three of those seven counts were for the deaths of the three captains—unlike in 1984, when Massino faced charges of *conspiracy* to murder for the triple homicide, this time around he was facing actual murder charges. And this time, he was convicted.) As the jury forewoman read the twenty-three-page verdict sheet, David Breitbart shook his head in disbelief. But Massino didn't have time for theatrics—moments later he was in Judge Garaufis' chamber spilling his guts, while Breitbart was standing outside the courthouse still claiming his client was innocent. Steve Dunleavy got his interview with Josephine and diligently reported her remarks. "Can you believe this is the United States of America?" she told Dunleavy. "It's like the old Soviet Union. No two stories from anyone on that stand matched. My husband wouldn't order anyone to hurt anyone."

* * *

Two months after Massino was found quilty, Agents Sallet and McCaffrey got a hot lead on a couple of guys Massino more than hurt. They drove out to a sodden, vacant lot on Ruby Street, Ozone Park, Queens, which would soon be blocked at both ends by police barricades. TV crews and print reporters clambered through bushes, trying to catch a glimpse of what was going on. In the distance they could make out a large backhoe systematically digging into the sloppy ground, removing scoops full of earth, old bricks and weeds.

The local residents filled the reporters in on the lot's sinister past. One lady reported to the *New York Times* that the lot had been a mob burial ground for fifty years. "One time, they found a guy with his tongue cut out," she said. Her urban legend wasn't quite accurate. The last time a dead mobster was found in that spot was only twenty-five years before, and he still had his tongue—he was Alphonse "Sonny Red" Indelicato. But somehow in 1981, when they removed Red's three-week-old corpse, the NYPD didn't bother to comb the rest of the lot. In 2004, fresh information emerged that said as many as four other bodies were buried beneath the surface. The newspapers speculated that one of them was John Favara, a Howard Beach furniture salesman who, in 1980, accidentally ran down John Gotti's twelve-year-old son, killing him. (Favara disappeared four months later, and was never seen again.) For days, Mafia-philes held their breath as agents from the FBI's Evidence Recovery Team unearthed a wristwatch, a pair of glasses, a human fibula, a tibia, part of a jawbone, ribs and a skull fragment. Six weeks later, we learned what agents McCaffrey and Sallet had believed all along: DNA testing revealed that the bodies belonged to Sonny Red's missing team members, Dominick "Big Trin" Trinchera and Philip "Phil Lucky" Giaccone.

For Greg Andres, the months leading up to Massino's trial had been the most hectic of his life. The chisel-faced prosecutor put in long, coffee-filled hours in his downtown Brooklyn office, his head buried in documents. He had to assemble and organize the evidence in the vast case against the mob boss. For years, it seemed like he'd done nothing but strategize, prepare court motions and spend hundreds of hours questioning the likes of Sal Vitale. Andres ate, breathed and (barely) slept the Massino case until his body ached. The wiry thirty-seven-year-old often commented that he could hardly wait until the trial was over, "so we can all get on with our lives." For that reason, the guilty verdicts for Joe Massino were more cause for relief than for celebration. At least, Andres thought they would be.

But in early 2005, people noticed that two plainclothes bodyguards had started shadowing Andres's every move. When he had to appear in court, the bodyguards (one of whom was a six-foot-plus woman) followed him in and sat close behind him. On paper, the prosecutor wasn't the type who needed protecting. He boxed at Notre Dame, and as a Peace Corps volunteer in West Africa, he survived two bouts of malaria. But the reason for the guard soon became clear: Andres's life was said to be in danger. He had allegedly been marked for death by none other than the Bonanno Crime Family, who wanted to rub out the brilliant young prosecutor before he nailed their boss on the still-pending death penalty murder case. The plot, however, had been foiled—the government had been tipped off, and the bodyguards scrambled into place. The source of that information? The last man Andres thought would ever help him. The man Andres had just put behind bars for good. The man the murder plot was supposed to be avenging.

Joseph C. Massino.

Splashed across New York's newspapers in January 2005 was a story the likes of which had never been seen, even in Mafia city. The *New York Post,* colorful as ever, screamed, "Mob Canary on Top Perch." The *Daily News* put it more bluntly: "Mob Boss a Rat." The city's headline writers had a new superlative to play with: the first-ever mob boss in New York's crime-ridden history had flipped. The Last Godfather was now working as an informant for the government.

In exchange for a reduced sentence on a still-pending murder charge against him—the murder of Gerlando "George from Canada" Sciascia—Joe Massino agreed to provide information about the alleged murder plot against Andres. Massino told the government he'd been approached by Vincent "Vinny Gorgeous" Basciano, the Family's acting boss, who offered to have Andres rubbed out. At the time, Basciano was behind bars, having been picked up on racketeering charges in November 2004. It was in the Brooklyn Federal Courthouse where Basciano and Massino allegedly crossed paths, and Basciano offered to have Andres killed. On

January 3, 2005, Massino was fitted with a recording device before the two men met again. As they spoke, Basciano admitted to having a Bonanno associate killed only weeks before. When Massino asked why, Basciano responded, "I thought this kid would be a good wake-up call for everybody." Four days later, Massino made another tape. (Basciano was later convicted for RICO conspiracy and got twenty years. He is still awaiting trial for the murder of the "kid," Randolph Pizzolo, a crime carrying the death penalty. Johnny Joe Spirito pled guilty to conspiracy to murder; Patty Defilippo was convicted at trial and got forty years.)

The news that Massino had ratted out his acting boss and exposed a plot to kill a prosecutor was met with universal shock on both sides of the law. It seemed impossible to believe that the same man who had so savagely defended the vow of *omertá* for so long was now betraying it. But in the face of so much treachery from his most trusted captains, Massino no longer had loyalty to anyone but himself. He was facing the death penalty for the 1999 murder of Sciascia and after being convicted on every count in the previous trial, his prospects of beating this next case were slim. He was on his way to becoming the first American mobster in a generation to be executed. So he took the only way out he could find: he gave the government Basciano, and then he told them, literally, where the bodies were buried.

At the old Brooklyn Federal Courthouse, the press corps sits in the jury box when high-profile prisoners are brought in for sentencing. Though in many ways fitting—the media passes judgment, wherever it sits—it's a tradition born of practicality. Because space in the public gallery benches is so limited on such occasions, there's nowhere else for reporters to sit. On the day of Joseph Massino's sentencing, when he would receive his term for the seven murders he had been convicted of carrying out, the jury box was full. Everyone from federal court beat writers to the city's famed, hard-nosed Mafia scribes had turned out. Among them were reporters who had covered every major mob trial from Crazy Joe Gallo to John Gotti: Author Jimmy Breslin sat between Jerry Capeci, the retired *Daily News* legend, and Juliet Papa, New York's very own voice of crime from radio 1010 WINS. We had a clear view of the front row of the courtroom, which had been reserved for family members. Sciascia's wife and daughter and Big Trin's family were the only ones willing to brave the media glare.

Massino entered from the side door, wearing the same steel-gray suit he had donned every day of the trial. As usual, he wasn't wearing a tie. He took his seat at the defense table beside his new lawyer, Edward McDonald. McDonald, the famous prosecutor-turned-defense attorney, who argued for the government in the Lufthansa heist case and who went so far as to play himself in the movie *Goodfellas,* had been secretly appointed shadow counsel by the judge after Massino flipped. The fact that Massino was cooperating was kept so hush-hush that one of his original attorneys, Flora Edwards, Breitbart's assistant at the trial, didn't even know she'd been replaced until the media broke the news. The deal was truly a coup for the government's Organized Crime Division: in his plea bargain, Massino agreed to testify for the government at a long list of future trials, where his intimate knowledge of the New York underworld could unmake dozens of made men. In exchange, the government agreed not to seek the death penalty for the Sciascia hit.

There was only one thing Massino couldn't avoid: he had to publicly own up to Sciascia's murder. It was an admission he was clearly uncomfortable making. He studiously avoided eye contact with his spectators in the courtroom, particularly the families of his victims. Judge Garaufis arrived, and invited the prosecution team, including Greg Andres, and the defense team to approach the bench. Then he asked Massino to say his piece. Seemingly at a loss for words, Massino turned to McDonald for direction and received a whispered instruction. "As boss of the Bonanno Family, I gave the order," Massino finally said, with his hands clasped around his middle. Not satisfied, Judge Garaufis asked for clarification. "And what was that?"

"To kill George from Canada."

Massino got two life sentences—half a life for every one that he ended—and an $8 million fine. Later that day, Josephine Massino—who played the devoted wife at every day of her husband's trial, but failed to show up for his sentencing—snuck into the courthouse to settle the restitution debt. The government let her keep the Howard Beach house, but she had to hand over what remained of the blood money. That afternoon, she signed away $7.6 million in cash and 267 gold bars worth one thousand dollars apiece.

Joseph Massino's reign over the city of New York ended as quietly as it had begun. After more than thirty years, at least eight murders, countless acts of violence, pain and loss, the Last Godfather got his chance to speak . . . and softly uttered just two sentences. "As the boss of the Bonanno Family, I gave the order . . . to kill George from Canada." That was it. There were no thunderclaps, no great fanfare, no rambling speeches about honor and secret societies. No apology, no remorse, not even rage. Nothing.

What had we been expecting? Why did Jimmy Breslin and I, and the rest of the reporters sitting nearby, feel as though we had been fooled? Here was the first New York mob boss ever to come clean, and he had virtually nothing to say for himself. What had gone wrong?

Looking back, the answer seems painfully obvious. Our expectation—and our desire—that Massino's big moment on the stand be filled with passion and revelation was fueled by our own fantasies. Judge Garaufis put it best in his closing remarks. "The activities, rituals and personalities of the world of organized crime have been deeply romanticized in the popular media over the past thirty years. However, this trial, like so many trials before it, has portrayed the true nature of organized crime." It was, in the end, just violence and greed, and Massino was just a man.

There will be many more trials, and many more gangsters brought down, especially now that the government has Massino under its thumb. But he won't bring them all down—hardworking agents like Sallet and McCaffrey and dedicated attorneys like Greg Andres will have to keep at it. They've certainly won a great battle, but not the war. And that's partly because of us. Hollywood's sugar-coated version of the Mafia has penetrated reality so much that, even as we vilify it, we crave more and more. As a society, we're fascinated by it. But that afternoon in a Brooklyn courtroom, we saw its true nature standing right before us with his head bowed. The Last Godfather was just a broken-down cook from Queens. Time will only tell who'll be the next Last Godfather, and who he will betray.

About the Author

Simon Crittle was born in Australia in 1970. After graduating university, he went to work for the *Sun-Herald* newspaper in Sydney. Like most cub reporters, he was given the police beat as his first assignment. During grueling graveyard shifts he'd fight to stay awake, listening to police frequencies on radio scanners. Occasionally, Simon chased an ambulance to a shooting or a freeway pileup and got his name on the front page. The long nights paid off as he built a reputation as one of the city's best crime reporters.

Photo by Toby Burrows

In 2000 Simon moved to New York, the world's crime capital, and landed a job at the *New York Post*. On September 11, the following year, his instinct for chasing sirens led him to the foot of the World Trade Center. His eyewitness report of the attack and his near-death experience led the paper the next day. He eventually left the *Post* to become the New York correspondent for *Time* magazine. It was there he spent a year investigating Joey Massino, the Last Godfather still operating in New York, and later turned the story into this book. Simon now works as a spokesman for the United Nations.

DEATH BY CANNIBAL

Criminals with an Appetite for Murder

PETER DAVIDSON

In these shocking true stories of
cannibalistic murder drawn from revealing
interviews with family members, authorities,
and the killers themselves, a veteran true
crime journalist profiles five American
cannibals, killers who hid behind masks
of normalcy and ate their victims:
Gary Heidnik, Albert Fentress,
John Weber, Nathaniel Bar-Jonah,
and Marc Sappington.

0-425-20741-2

**Available wherever books are sold or at
penguin.com**

TRUE CRIME FROM BERKLEY BOOKS

A BEAUTIFUL CHILD
*A True Story of Hope, Horror, and an
Enduring Human Spirit*
by Matt Birkbeck
0-425-20440-5
**The tragic, true story of the girl-next-door's
secret life.**

UNBRIDLED RAGE
*A True Story of Organized Crime, Corruption,
and Murder in Chicago*
by Gene O'Shea
0-425-20526-2
**Two cold case agents solve the mystery of the
40-year-old murder of three boys in Chicago.**

ON THE HOUSE
The Bizarre Killing of Michael Malloy
by Simon Read
0-425-20678-5
**The true story of the murder of a New York City
drunk at the hands of thugs who had taken out
an insurance policy on his life.**

HUNTING ERIC RUDOLPH
*An Insider's Account of the Five-Year Search for the
Olympic Bomber*
by Henry Schuster with Charles Stone
0-425-20857-5
**The definitive story of the hunt for the elusive
suspect in the 1996 Atlanta Olympic bombing.**

Penguin Group (USA) Online

What will you be reading tomorrow?

Tom Clancy, Patricia Cornwell, W.E.B. Griffin,
Nora Roberts, William Gibson, Robin Cook,
Brian Jacques, Catherine Coulter, Stephen King,
Dean Koontz, Ken Follett, Clive Cussler,
Eric Jerome Dickey, John Sandford,
Terry McMillan, Sue Monk Kidd, Amy Tan,
John Berendt…

You'll find them all at
penguin.com

Read excerpts and newsletters,
find tour schedules and reading group guides,
and enter contests.

Subscribe to Penguin Group (USA) newsletters
and get an exclusive inside look
at exciting new titles and the authors you love
long before everyone else does.

PENGUIN GROUP (USA)
us.penguingroup.com